TRUE IDENTITY

TRUE IDENTITY

A SPIRITUAL POETRY INHERITANCE

INDIA C. WILSON

WITHIN US IS THE KINGDOM

iUniverse, Inc.
Bloomington

TRUE IDENTITY
A Spiritual Poetry Inheritance

iUniverse books may be ordered through booksellers or by contacting:

iUniverse
1663 Liberty Drive
Bloomington, IN 47403
www.iuniverse.com
1-800-Authors (1-800-288-4677)

ISBN: 978-1-4759-4811-0 (sc)
ISBN: 978-1-4759-4813-4 (hc)
ISBN: 978-1-4759-4812-7 (e)

Library of Congress Control Number: 2012916452

Printed in the United States of America

iUniverse rev. date: 09/19/2012

DEDICATED TO MY ROYAL SEEDS

POEMS BY INDIA WILSON
EDITED BY COREY WILSON
ART (PENCIL DRAWINGS) BY DANTE' WILSON

HONORING AND THANKING MY

HEAVENLY FATHER

Introduction

"True Identity" is written in narrative poetry form to reveal its uniqueness. "True Identity" shares a spiritual enlightenment and heritage awakening through characters in a personal story, poetry, art, bible scriptures and images. The story begins with the end of one journey that leads to a spiritual awakening into the next.

I start my poetic journey with a short American saga because the saga awakened the strength that I already had. I allowed another to control my destiny and temporary lost myself in the dreams of another but through spiritual enlightenment I found my True Identity.

"True Identity" is not your average book of poetry because the poetry is connected to the stories, biblical scriptures, art and images.

Since I was a little girl, I was into poetry. I wrote about everything that I saw going on. Why? I was trying to understand this world that we live in. I was trying to understand the who, what, why, when, where and how. I feel that we must seek truth. Our life, our true identity! Most races can trace their history but we (so-called Blacks) hold on to the voyage of slavery as if that's our only legacy. Well, I'm here to tell you-it's not my friend.

Queen India at 49

It's sociologically important for us (the so called black race) to know our true identity because it affects our moral fiber, social mobility, and total well-being. Not knowing our true history changes our nature into one that is not our own. It changes the way we see and know ourselves–the way we see others and our reaction to life and all of its demands on us. Knowing will enrich our soul to reach our highest heights and live and perform at our utmost ability, thereby strengthening every aspect of our moral fiber and greatly improving our well-being and the way we interact with the world.

TABLE OF CONTENTS

CHAPTER 1
REFLECTIONS

AMERICAN SAGA:

It's the 4th day of the week and I have a big date with my boyfriend Marcus at San-Delo Italian Restaurant. I truly care about him a lot. He is exactly what I want. I mean the brother is fine yawl and... he has a nice job!

Uh Oh!

I really hope he is not mad at me for being 15 minutes late.

Look, I know what you're probably thinking right now;

Girl, do not be late for your big date! Why are you making that man wait? Don't worry. I'm not at home or stuck in traffic. I'm in San-Delo's restroom checking myself out.

Hey, a girl has got to make sure she looks good.

Plus, he told me there's no rush because tonight is a special night for the both of us. It's our 5 year anniversary of being together. I hope he pop the big question that I've been waiting years for.

I'm standing in front of the bathroom mirror staring at my reflection.

What do I see? I see: a thirty-four year old woman ready for true Love. I'm so excited! I can't believe the wait is finally over. I walk out of the ladies room and take a deep breath.

(I Breath)

Here goes nothing!

As I walk straight to the dining table, I see my prince charming standing up waiting for his princess.

He then says to me...

Marcus - Wow! You look beautiful!

India - Thank you sweetie. Hee, hee (laughter).

Marcus - You're so silly. Hold up baby girl, wait right here. Do not move a muscle!

(He walks towards my chair and pulls it open)

India - Oh wow! Thank you for pulling my chair out for me. "You are way to kind" ha, ha, ha, ha (laughter).

Marcus - No problem! What's so funny? (He scratches his head)

India - I don't know. It's just that you're acting extra sweet tonight.

Marcus - Well tonight is a special night for me. I mean for us!

India – Aw isn't that sweet. You definitely went the extra mile this time. I mean San-Delo's? Marcus you didn't have to do this! Only rich people come to this place.

Marcus - And that's what I'm going to be pretty soon. (he smiles)

India – Honey you know none of that stuff matters to me. I love you for you.

Marcus – Aw yes I know... Look India I have something I want to talk to you about.

{Marcus then gets down on his knees and holds my hand}

India – Oh wow!

YES MARCUS, I WILL MARRY YOU!

(PEOPLE BEGIN TO CHEER)

Marcus – Whoa! India, why are you saying that? I hope you're not thinking that's why we are here.

{I laugh it off}

India - Well yes-- It has been 5 years Marcus, but it's ok. I'll wait for you as long as it takes. Anyway, don't you think it's time for our relationship to get an upgrade?

{Marcus starts shaking his head}

Marcus – India, why are you being so selfish?

India – Honey I'm not and why are you talking to me like that? Is there something wrong?

Marcus – Yes there is! I don't want to marry you!

{Huh}

Marcus - In fact, I never planned on it. India, I brought you here to tell you that I am not happy!

India – How is that so? I thought everything was going wonderful. Wait a minute! If you're not proposing to me, why are you holding my hand on the floor?

Marcus – India, can't you see I'm trying to end this relationship as gentle as possible. I'm not ready to be in a relationship. I have too many goals that I must accomplish and I don't want anyone standing in the way of them.

{I take a second to breathe}

India – Marcus, I can't believe you just said that. Are you trying to tell me I'm standing in the way of your happiness?

Marcus – Look…that is not what I'm saying, so why are you making this harder on yourself?

{I take a deep breath}

Marcus – India, I also brought you here to tell you I'm moving. Tomorrow is my last chance to move to Paris! I can finally have a fresh start. I was offered a really great job over there.

{I begin to cry}

Marcus – Aw come on, don't cry! Can't you see; this works out for the best. You finally get the time you need to write your book without me taking all of your attention. You know I was never into that "power to the people" stuff.

India – Power to the people! Really Marcus, is that how you see me? And please don't mention my book; it has nothing to do with this and you know it.

Marcus – India, Why are your causing a scene?

India – WHY? Think about it! After 5 years of catering to you and loving you, you're finally going to bring me to a nice restaurant to tell me you're not happy.

{I grab a bottle of champagne and shake it real hard}

Marcus - Now honey, don't do that!

India - What Marcus, embarrass you? How are you going to just up and leave me like this? I thought you loved me.

Marcus – Look, it's too late for all of that. My stuff will be gone by noon tomorrow.

India - Noon? Marcus you know I can't afford that house alone.

Marcus – Look, don't worry about that. I got you covered for a few months.

{I begin to have a reality check}

India - So you mean I was living in sin, going against my spirituality and thinking you were going to marry me? Instead you use me and walk away. Wow, you are a classic jerk!

{I then pop the bottle of champagne and shower his face with it}

Marcus - Yeah that's real classy India, real classy!

{Marcus then takes a napkin and wipes the champagne off his face}

Marcus – India, I'm sorry it had to end this way.

THE WAIT

Together for such a long time
You think we would be in a serene state of mind
United – Together as one
Happiness and bliss under the sun

...

Thinking that a change is going to come
Thinking I would officially be his wife
The pain is as if cut with a knife
Being used galore and making me wait
Thinking a life with him was my fate

...

Equally yoked, No need to beg for a hand in marriage
Year after year, waiting for the union
Not knowing you are his illusion

...

Putting him on a pedestal
Making him our everything
Forgetting that our Heavenly Father only holds that role
Forgetting ourselves and almost losing our soul

...

Trying to please another while waiting for them to shine
No Love, blinded by lust and desire, not safe
Deception, betrayal, lust and lies
We all have alibis
Maybe the thought of loneliness
I must escape this place and release myself from the wait

{I LATER ARRIVE HOME ALONE}

I kicked my shoes by the front door and ran straight upstairs. I flopped on the bed crying a river; hoping that sleep would ease the pain but I could not sleep. Maybe one of my African movies will help me forget my worries. They have some of the best actors and actresses in the world. I need something to wipe these tears away.

This is the last time...the last call...

THE LAST CALL

When I said it was the last call
It was because it was the last fall
The last time I would experience such mess
The last time I would settle for less

...

Ups and downs
Year after year
Filling up napkins with tear after tear

...

Oh, I don't think I can cry anymore
It's the last call for the fool I left outside my door

...

Wondering why I remained in this deep sleep
It took years before my awakening
For my soul I wanted to keep

...

It was the last time I pulled the smallest straw
For my hopes and dreams I already saw
A glimpse into spiritual reality
It was more than just a mere formality
For they said because of my suffering
My future would be blessed
Look at you, you already shine
Your last call from your last fall has made you divine

CHAPTER 2
FREEING OUR HERITAGE

Why does it hurt so bad? You know break ups... I should have seen this coming a long time ago but I was blinded by a lie. I should have seen the signs. He never let me speak my mind. I always wanted to share the truth of who we really are with him but he always cut me off. He would always tell me to leave the past alone and live in the 21th century.

In him, I forgot that I was beautiful, young and intelligent. I forgot about my talents and gifts. I put my spiritual self on the shelf for him. I conformed to what he wanted me to be. I was in his twilight-zone. Not knowing that my Heavenly Father would set me free.

Heritage Breakdown

A breakdown of our heritage is needed right away
Don't you know how much they have stolen and taken away
We have family that we see everyday
Not knowing who they are, the hate goes each way

...

Have you ever heard of the Lost Tribes of Israel
Our history is not that of slavery and cotton gins
Read the Holy Bible
In it you will win

...

Shem, Ham and Japheth (sons of Noah) populated the world after
the flood
It's in the Bible
Haven't you heard
Read it in Genesis, Chapter 10 and 11,
Yes, That's the word

- Out of Shem were the Hebrews (Abraham, Isaac, Jacob
  {Israel/So-called Blacks})
- Out of Japheth were the Asians
- Out of Ham were the Africans

We (So called Blacks/Negros) come from Shem not Ham!

Don't be confused because color does not show your relation. For
the chosen Tribe of Israel suffered on every occasion.

The Bible tells us how we (So-called Blacks/Negros) were brought
here (America) on ships. You know the rest. Yes; Our ancestors
beaten with whips. Only the Tribe of Judah (Jacob/Israel seeds

AKA Negros) were treated this way. Continue your research; what more can I say?

Check out the 12 Tribes of Israel (Judah, Reuben, Simeon, Levi, Dan, Naphtali, Gad, Asher, Issachar, Zebulun, Joseph and Benjamin) when you research. The Bible tells us how the false Jewish people that control our homeland today are not who they claim they are. Read this verse and get the news:

Revelation 2:9 I know thy works, and tribulation, and poverty, (but thou art rich) and I know the blasphemy of them which say they are Jews, and are not, but are the synagogue of Satan.

Who worship in synagogues? He made it clear. He knows our works, tribulation and poverty. He knows about the blasphemy of them that are not. He knows all of Satan's plots.

WAKE UP
(Scriptures to Wake you Up)

Genesis 15: 13 And he said unto Abram, know of a surety that thy seed shall be a stranger in a land that is not theirs, and shall serve them; and they shall afflict them four hundred years; 14 And also that nation, whom they shall serve, will I judge: and afterward shall they come out with great substance. 15 And though shalt go to thy fathers in peace; thou shalt be buried in a good old age. 16 But in the fourth generation they shall come hither again for the iniquity of the Amorites is not yet full.

Exodus 13: 3 And Moses said unto the people, Remember this day, in which ye came out from Egypt, out of the house of bondage; for by strength of hand the LORD brought you out from this place: there shall no leavened bread be eaten.

Deuteronomy 28: 68 And the LORD shall bring thee into Egypt again with ships, by the way whereof I spake unto thee, Thou shalt see it no more again: and there ye shall be sold unto your enemies for bondmen and bondwomen, and no man shall buy you.

The only time in history a people were
brought in on ships in great masses
Was during Negro slavery
They suffered and died but all through bravery

Our second Egypt is America
Who my people were brought here on ships
Who were sold unto their enemies
Our so called Colored, Negroes, Black/African American
Tampered with
Yes
But what our Heavenly Father wants us to know is in the Bible
Don't let internet propaganda/media
Nor literature, photos, bones etc. deceive you
What they didn't know was that the Bible repeats itself
They could not wipe our entire history out
Although they tried through his story/their story
Continue the research - Bring out what is true

<u>CHOSEN</u>

How wonderful and blessed to have such an anointed one
Our Creator loved us so much
Although we sinned he still sent us his son
To teach us, To love us
To carry us to the light
To help us understand that we must do right

...

Follow his teachings and we shall see
Everlasting joy and eternity
They changed his name and his physical appearance
They can't take the truth because it is within us

...

Turn down your music.
Don't go dancing tonight
No arguing or fighting
No cards or Bud-light

...

Open your bible in quiet delight
Read for yourself for your spirit shall light
He is about peace and healing the soul
Blessing the meek while we gracefully grow old
There is no one to blame if you turn away from him with might
He wants you, even in your darkest night

...

Your soul shall be saved - True peace at last
Our Messiah loves us
In-spite of our past
We are blessed with the greatest gift of all
Our heritage, our birthright, We are Israel

We must read our Bible - For we shall see
Israel is you and me
Blood of his Blood - We are the chosen ones
Read with understanding because our life has just begun

Psalm 135: 4 For the LORD hath chosen Jacob unto himself, and Israel for his peculiar treasure.

AWAKEN

Awaken - You're the one
Awaken - He gave his son
He's the greatest
He made the Hebrew Israelites the Chosen

...

Live your life for our Father in Heaven
Positive choices
Stay away from negative voices
Leading you astray
Trying to delete the word
The Bible
The original source
Where do you think Hollywood and the media got their voice

...

Whatever suffering you may endure
Stand assure that you are secure, Awaken
Living your life trusting in our Heavenly Father
Believing in his son
Saving you has just begun, Awaken

...

Delivering me from the evil one
No weapon formed against me shall prosper
Supernatural perseverance
Protected by the Heavens
Even through the pain
Joy in Heaven I have gained
Prayers up to heaven in my darkest hours
Has saved my soul
Bringing me closer, Awaken

...

Leaving my ills, chills and all of the discomforts
For this new life with my King
Blessings to our Heavenly Father
Knowing that I have peace
Because I am chosen and have Awaken

Yes! We must continue to free our heritage from the wraths of slavery. If you don't remember... check out our tragedy:

ABOARD AN ARAB SLAVE SHIP INTERCEPTED BY THE ROYAL NAVY, 1869

PUBLIC DOMAIN

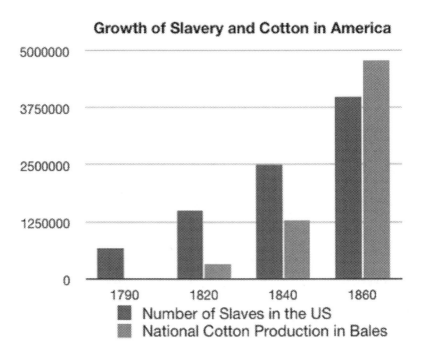

Growth of Slavery and Cotton in America

■ Number of Slaves in the US
■ National Cotton Production in Bales

$100 REWARD !

Ranaway from Richards' Ferry, Culpeper County, Va., 23rd instant, ABRAM, who is about 30 years old, 5 feet from 8 to 10 inches high, and weighs from 175 to 180. His complexion is dark, though not black, and hair long for a negro. He is a very shrewd fellow, and there is reason to believe he is attempting to get to a free State. I will give the above Reward if taken out of Virginia--$50 if taken 20 miles from home, or $20 if taken in the neighborhood. WM. T. J. RICHARDS, *Adm'r of Jas. Richards, Dec'd.*
Sept. 24.

<u>Psalm 83: 3</u> They have taken crafty counsel against thy people, and consulted against thy hidden ones. 4 They have said, Come, and let us cut them off from being a nation; that the name of Israel may be no more in remembrance.

Deuteronomy 28: 15 But it shall come to pass, if thou wilt not hearken unto the voice of the LORD thy God, to observe to do all his commandments and his statutes which I command thee this day; that all these curses shall come upon thee, and overtake thee: 16 Cursed shalt thou be in the city, and cursed shalt though be in the field. 17 Cursed shall be thy basket and thy store. 18 Cursed shall be the fruit of thy body, and the fruit of thy land, the increase of thy kine, and the flocks of thy sheep. 19 Cursed shall thy be when thou comest in, and cursed shalt thou be when thou goest out. 25 The LORD shall cause thee to be smitten before thine enemies: thou shalt go out one way against them, and flee seven ways before them: and shalt be removed into all the kingdoms of the earth.

VALUABLE GANG OF YOUNG

NEGROES

By JOS. A. BEARD.

Will be sold at Auction,

ON WEDNESDAY, 25TH INST.

At 12 o'clock, at Banks' Arcade,

17 Valuable Young Negroes, Men and Women, Field Hands. Sold for no fault; with the best city guarantees.

Sale Positive and without reserve!

☞TERMS CASH.

New Orleans, March 24, 1840.

PUBLIC DOMAIN

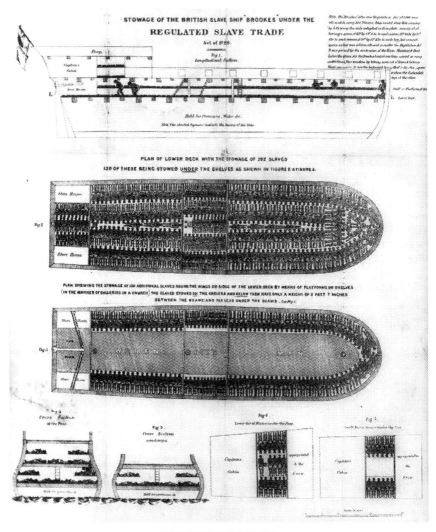

<u>Deuteronomy 28: 68</u> And the LORD shall bring thee into Egypt <u>again</u> with <u>ships,</u> by the way whereof I spake unto thee, Thou shalt see it no more again: and there ye shall be <u>sold unto your enemies</u> for bondmen and bondwomen, and no man shall <u>buy</u> you.

Notice: The word <u>buy</u> underlined meaning redeem: to free from what distresses or harms.

THE NEW SLAVE PLANTATION

Prison - My darling is the new slave plantation for true
They call it jail while they still subjugate you
Toilets by the bed
Lead in your head from the falling paint
Prison guards guarding - But none really saints
Messing with your mind
On lock down all the time
Nothing healthy about your meal
Makes your stomach strong as steal
While you plan and plot to control that meal and a cot
It will cost you a lot
Just to piss in the toilet that's next to your cot
Muslim, Christian or Aryan-nation
You need to join one to protect your sacred creation
They control the lot - They control your plots
They even control your conversations
The new slave plantation is full of segregation
Prison is where they want to keep you
Ignorance is how they still beat you
Knowledge is the power that will release your soul
Your Heavenly Father can release their hold
Shame keeps you down
Lust has no bound
Flesh will destroy your very core
Crack, weed or whatever the crime

They developed a new reason for your plantation time
Tyrone told you he got caught
Mike told you he got bought
But you still said - "No not me"
Now you are serving plantation time
Calling relatives and friends
Draining their every dime
You've heard the commercials that "Crime don't pay"
You ignored it for the slave plantation that's everyday

NO - NOT MY GOODIES

No - Not my goodies
I'm wearing hoodies everyday

...

Pants sagging
My walks dragging
I'm pimpin every step of the way

...

I control this cell
I create all of my smells
I am the master of me

...

But when Big Joe comes around
All walls are down and my goodies he wants to see

...

No - Not my goodies
I can't go out like that
I have a beautiful wife at home

...

What will I tell her of this shame that I've met
A secret
I will keep in my mind, I will forget
No - Why my goodies
I am a real man
I don't understand what this place has done to my mind
No longer fearing
No longer hearing the voice from the Most High
People are swearing - People not caring what they do or say
Now - Reading Revelations in the end - We all will have to pay

WAITING FOR MY MAN

I'm waiting for my man
He's on lock down for a while
I am seven months pregnant with our third male child
He's coming home real soon
We never had a honey-moon
Maybe we will celebrate then

...

My girlfriend told me he had some trouble the other day
With some guy name Big Joe
Her man's in the cell down two rows
You know how gossip flows

...

I spoke to him about it - Don't worry he said
Nothing but a misunderstanding
It didn't sound right
I can't sleep tonight
What is the message he's sending

...

I'm waiting for my man and I don't understand
Why does he have to lie to me
The news of his event was not only girlfriend sent but all over the
infirmary

...

Still waiting for my man with his new son in my hands
Wondering how life is going to be
His spirits been taken
His manhood shaken
No more celebration for me

...

I went to see him the other day
I could tell Big Joe was up his way
No more will I have to wait
No more waiting for the man
That once held me in his hand
For the plantation took him away
A slave they made him
Big Joe betrayed him and led his soul astray

INNOCENT

Innocent until proven guilty is what I believed
Handcuffs and bars is what I received

...

I don't know that woman - I have never seen her face before
I am celibate and pure - I practice what I preach for sure

...

Every skin that's dark - Don't snatch up women in the park
Nor do we hurt them

...

We don't all sell drugs nor go to clubs
There are millions of great Black men

...

Innocent you will see
The Creator will protect me
My soul belongs to him

...

Your cuffs and bars
Your clubs and jars
Or whatever poison you want to feed me

...

My innocence lies in my soul
Justice the Creator holds
The truth in the end - The Messiah will unfold

Innocent

Revelation 2:10 Fear none of those things which thou shalt suffer: behold, the devil shall cast some of you into prison, that ye may be tried; and ye shall have tribulation ten days: be thou faithful unto death, and I will give thee a crown of life.

INNOCENT

PENCIL ART BY DANTE' WILSON

Deuteronomy 28: 25 The LORD shall cause thee to be smitten before thine enemies: thou shalt go out one way against them, and flee seven ways before them: and shalt be removed into all the kingdoms of the earth. 37 And thou shalt become an astonishment, a proverb, and a byword, among all nations whither the LORD shall lead thee. 48 Therefore shalt though serve thine enemies which the LORD shall send against thee, in hunger, and in thirst, and in nakedness, and in want of all things: and he shall put a yoke of iron upon thy neck, until he have destroyed thee. 49 The LORD shall bring a nation against thee from far, from the end of the earth, as swift as the eagle flieth; a nation whose tongue thou shalt not understand; 50 A nation of fierce countenance, which shall not regard the person of the old, nor show favour to the young: 64 And the LORD shall scatter thee among all people, from the one end of the earth even unto the other; and there thou shalt serve other gods, which neither thou nor thy fathers have known, even wood and stone. 65 And among these nations shalt thou find no ease, neither shall the sole of thy foot have rest: but the LORD shall give thee there a trembling heart, and failing of eyes, and sorrow of mind.

Deuteronomy 29: 24 Even all nations shall say, Wherefore hath the LORD done thus unto this land? What meaneth the heat of this great anger? 25 Then men shall say, <u>Because they have forsaken the covenant of the LORD God of their fathers, which he made with them when he brought them forth out of the land of Egypt: 26 For they went and served other gods, and worshiped them, gods whom they knew not, and whom he had not given unto them: 27 And the anger of the LORD was kindled against this land, to bring upon it all the curses that are written in this book: 28 And the LORD rooted them out of their land in anger, and in wrath, and in great indignation, and cast them into another land, as it is this day</u>.

Jeremiah 3: 18 In those days the house of Judah shall walk with the house of Israel, and they shall come together out of the land of the north to the land that I have given for an inheritance unto your fathers.

Jeremiah 12: 14 <u>Thus saith the LORD against all mine evil neighbours, that touch the inheritance which I have caused my people Israel to inherit; Behold, I will pluck them out of their land, and pluck out the house of Judah from among them. 15 And it shall come to pass, after that I have plucked them out I will return, and have compassion on them, and will bring them again, every man to his heritage, and every man to his land</u>.

Matthew 2: 13 And when they were departed, behold, the angel of the Lord appeared to Joseph in a dream, saying, Arise, and take the young child and his mother, and flee into Egypt, and be thou there until I bring thee word: for Herod will seek the young child to destroy him.

NOTE: Joseph took our savior (as a young child) to a Black Egypt to hide. How could that be done with a blonde haired/blue eyed Jesus as they portray in the photos?

Revelation 1: 14 His head and his hairs were white like wool, as white as snow; and his eyes were as a flame of fire; 15 And his feet like unto fine brass, as if they burned in a furnace; and his voice as the sound of many waters.

Joel 3: 1 For, behold, in those days, and in that time, when I shall bring again the captivity of Judah and Jerusalem, 2 I will also gather all nations, and will bring them down into the valley of Jehoshaphat, and will plead with them there for my people and for my heritage Israel, whom they have scattered among the nations, and parted my land. 3 And they have cast lots for my people; and have given a boy for an harlot, and sold a girl for wine, that they might drink. 6 The children also of Judah and the children of Jerusalem have ye sold unto the Grecians, that ye might remove them far from their border. 7 <u>Behold, I will raise them out of the place whither ye have sold them, and will return your recompense upon your own head:</u>

Joel 3: 8 <u>And I will sell your sons and your daughters into the hand of the children of Judah, and they shall sell them to the Sabeans, to a people far off: for the LORD hath spoken it. 16 The LORD also shall roar out of Zion, and utter his voice from Jerusalem; and the heavens and the earth shall shake but the Lord will be the hope of his people, and the strength of the children of Israel.</u>

Lamentations 5:7 Our fathers have sinned, and are not; and we have borne their iniquities. 8 Servants have ruled over us: there is none that doth deliver us out of their hand. 9 We gat our bread with the peril of our lives because of the sword of the wilderness. 10 Our skin was black like an oven because of the terrible famine. 11 They ravished the women in Zion, and the maids in the cities of Judah. 12 Princes are hanged up by their hand: the faces of elders were not honoured. 13 They took the young men to grind, and the children fell under the wood.

Amos 9:7 Are ye not as children of the Ethiopians unto me, O children of Israel? saith the LORD. Have not I brought up Israel out of the land of Egypt? And the Philistines from Caphtor, and the Syrians from Kir? 8 Behold, the eyes of the Lord GOD are upon the sinful kingdom, and I will destroy it from off the face of the earth; saving that I will not utterly destroy the house of Jacob, saith the LORD. 10 <u>All the sinners of my people shall die by the sword, which say, The evil shall not overtake nor prevent us. 11 In that day I raise up the tabernacle of David</u>

that is fallen, and close the breaches thereof; and I will raise up his ruins, and I will build it as in the days of old; 14 And I will bring again the captivity of my people of Israel, and they shall build the waste cities, and inhabit them; and they shall plant vineyards and drink the wine thereof; they shall also make gardens and eat the fruit of them. 15 And I will plant them upon their land, and they shall no more be pulled up out of their land which I have given them saith the LORD thy God.

Zechariah 8: 7 Thus saith the LORD of host; Behold, I will save my people from the east country, and from the west country.

Zephaniah 3: 10 From beyond the rivers of Ethiopia my suppliants, even the daughter of my dispersed, shall bring mine offering.

John 8: 32 And ye shall know the truth, and the truth shall make you free.

UNITED

United we shall stand because divided we have fallen
The voices of our ancestors is spiritually calling
Calling for a change so that we can lift up every voice
United Israel, you still have a choice

JUDAH: Judah was Jacob's (Israel's) fourth son. The Messiah (Savior) was born out of the Tribe of Judah and is the descendant of Judah. The term Jew came from the name Judah which denotes a family lineage/ethnicity but not a religion. Our Messiah (Savior) was a Jew by blood not religion like the Jewish people today. The Jewish people of today do not demonstrate the culture, values nor customs of the biblical Jews and they do not uphold the laws of Moses. Their history and physical description does not match the prophecies of the Old Testament Jews. Let it be known that the Jewish people (Khazars) of today have no historical claim to the land of Israel. They have controlled and monopolized the media, our education system and the textbook industry. This has been done to keep us (AKA Blacks/Tribes of Israel) in ignorance of our true identity. Wake up my people, Wake up!

When you look at the so-called Blacks with our many different features from the shapes of our heads, eyes, nose and tones in our skin; you are looking at the different tribes of Israel clustered together that were kidnaped and sold into slavery. African Americans are from a holy bloodline that has been scattered throughout the world. The Jewish people that we see in Egypt today are not the Jews that we read about in the Bible. Their race is Caucasian (Turks) and they are Jewish by religion. The slave trade was heavily, but not solely, financed by the Jewish (Khazars) people of today that stole our birthright and identity.

Revelation 2:9 I know thy works, and tribulation, and poverty, (but though art rich) and I know the blasphemy of them which say they are Jews, and are not, but are the synagogue of Satan. 10 Fear none of those things which thou shalt suffer; behold, the devil shall cast some of you into prison, that ye may be tried; and ye shall have tribulation ten days; be thou faithful unto death, and I will give thee a crown of life. 11 He that hath an ear, let him hear what the Spirit saith unto the churches; He that overcometh shall not be hurt of the second death.

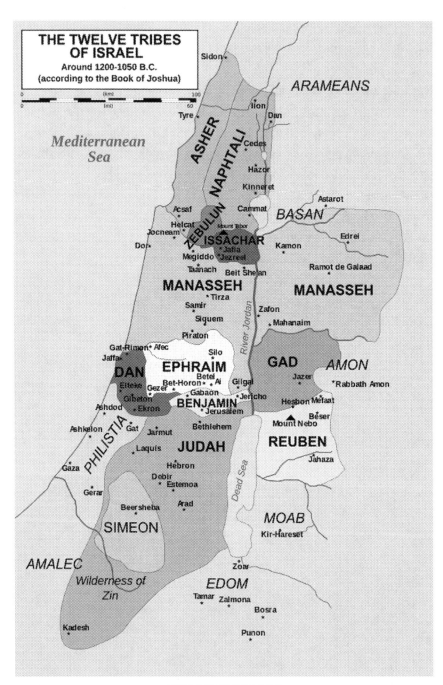

THE TWELVE TRIBES
OF ISRAEL
Around 1200-1050 B.C.
(according to the Book of Joshua)

Mediterranean
Sea

ARAMEANS

Sidon
Tyre
Lion
Dan

ASHER
NAPHTALI
Cedes
Hazor
Kinneret
Astarot
Acsaf
Cammat
BASAN
Helcat
Mount Tabor
Jocneam
ZEBULUN
ISSACHAR
Edrei
Dor
Jafia
Kamon
Megiddo
Jezreel
Taanach
Beit Shelan
Ramot de Galaad
MANASSEH
Tirza
MANASSEH
Samir
Zafon
Siquem
Mahanaim
Piraton
River Jordan
Gat-Rimon
Afec
Silo
Jaffa
EPHRAIM
GAD
AMON
DAN
Betel
Bet-Horon
Ai
Gilgal
Jazer
Rabbath Amon
Elteke
Gezer
Gabaon
Jericho
Gibeton
BENJAMIN
Hesbon
Melaat
Ashdod
Ekron
Jerusalem
Beser
Ashkelon
Gat
Jarmut
Bethlehem
Mount Nebo
Laquis
JUDAH
REUBEN
Jahaza
Gaza
Hebron
Debir
Estemoa
Gerar
Dead Sea
Beersheba
Arad
MOAB
SIMEON
Kir-Hareset
AMALEC
Zoar
Wilderness of
Zin
EDOM
Tamar
Zalmona
Bosra
Kadesh
Punon

AFRICAN AMERICAN?

African American? (What!) America was named after an Italian map reader/alleged explorer in approximately 1507: Amerigo Vespucci was born in Florence, Italy in 1454. He helped Christopher Columbus get ships ready for voyages to the New World. Amerigo's name was given to North and South America because he was allegedly the first to learn that it was not a part of Asia. He allegedly explored what we now call North and South America in approximately 1497.

This book is meant to help you use your Creator given talents. Continue your research. I have only touched on a small portion of our rich and royal heritage. I pray that you seek so that you can find the many truths that are out here. You will stumble on a lot that will throw you overboard but pray and fast and ask our Heavenly Father to lead your way in your quest for the truth.

John 8: 32 And ye shall know the truth, and the truth shall make you free.

***** Our Heavenly Father's love is evident everywhere. Our Creator is about love. I am about love. My gift is for you to know your true identity and to love and respect yourself. By knowing yourself, you will be able to effectively communicate with all races and use wisdom when sharing your knowledge. Remember, knowledge is not arrogance. Stay peaceful and flee from sin.

CHAPTER 3
COLOR AND
HAIR EPISODE

(((THINKING ABOUT MARCUS)))

The signs were in my face. I just made excuses for him. Marcus always complained when I talked about going natural with my hair.

Perm, wig or weave—He did not care; as long as it wasn't natural. He hated it when I wore my beautiful head wraps and coverings. He always got upset when I spent too much time in the sun. He would say: "I don't date anyone darker than me."

I thought he was joking when he made those types of statements. I was so into him that I did not see the writing on the wall.

I use to tell him: "The darker the berry the sweeter the juice." He would respond with: "I don't like my juice Sweet!" It was as if He was ashamed of being a person of color.

There were times when he acted like a:

House Negro

A house Negro told me not to write this book
He said he feared for my life
For the words are hooks (connection)
A hook to release Blacks (Israelites) from the chains and the crooks
For he was fearful because of the truth - Lives are took
He said he was brought in as a witness - He seen it the other day
He held their demise in silence and went on about his way
I told him that I understood and know the truth in what he was saying
But the souls and life of our people are being slain

...

I told him that it was a part of my destiny to release this Poetical Truth
To educate my people to release their Identity Proof
I told him that the Creator watches over me
That everyone involved - If I'm hurt
The Creator will eventually annihilate

...

When we live in fear
We are not truly living
When we hide our knowledge
We give others power

...

Power to control
Power to take hold
Power to dictate our every move
Power to destroy and have our people living like fools
Not know
Not showing
Not living our true self worth
Ignorant of the knowledge of our true genius and royal birth

WHY AM I SO DARK?

Why am I so dark
You are blessed my child - So your beauty must shine

...

Shine like the diamond that we treasure so much
Remarkable in appearance with radiance you shine
Your darkness my child is truly divine

...

Shades of Bronze from the earth to the Core
Your beauty is such as never before
Love the skin you are in for none come without sin but the Messiah
For your dark skin will take you higher

...

Higher in truth - Knowing who you are
Never second guessing that you are a shining star

...

Be pure in heart and follow our Creator's lead
For you are chosen
You come from our Heavenly Father's seed

...

Your darkness will protect you from the rays of the sun
For your homeland is hot and one day you will return

...

Our health came in to mind when he made us this way
Our darkness gives us strength to endure the Evil one's slay

...

Never doubt your color for you are just like the Messiah
You shine throughout the Earth
You are an eloquent being
Look again in the mirror and respect and love what you are seeing

ASHAMED OF YOUR COLOR

Ashamed of your color so you want the white baby doll
Not knowing your beauty
That you are the true cutie and your darkness makes you unique
Golden brown, chocolate divine, caramel with sweet flavor
It's your beauty that is envied
Why do you think they fry and burn on the sun-tan table
See the beauty in yourself and stop wanting to be another
Look at your true state are you ashamed of your own mother
No matter how white your doll
She will be your down fall
For that mindset will grow in your nature
Our Heavenly Father is our Creator
He designed us in his own image
Why do you question his design
Insecure of your color - Refresh your own mind
Television, magazines, all media can show you
What they have created as beauty
Look at yourself
Know your own worth
It's your everyday duty
Holding that white doll will not get you the rich white man
Holding that white doll will not get you love from the whites
Holding that white doll will not make you white
What holding that white doll will get you is a depletion of your
created birth
Holding that white doll will take away your self-worth
Thinking you have to have white to be right
Thinking that the white man is your true knight

Growing up not wanting a baby that look like you
Lightening your race is that your cure
So you have the white baby but your face is still black
Racism still remains - They still tell you to take 3 steps back
Having that white baby did not change the way they treat your color
Do you feel prettier now because you are a white baby's mother
White baby's mother your beauty is still true
Although white, that baby is still just a little Black you

DARK SKIN COLOR - THE LINGUISTIC MYSTERY

The Egyptologist Cheikh Anta Diop; invented a method for determining the level of melanin in the skin of human beings. He conducted the method on Egyptian mummies in the Museum of Man in Paris. Cheikh Anta Diop's test indicated that the remains were of Black people.

I won't say it twice
But I will preach it once
That it was color from the very beginning
So your visual perception - Should be one that is award winning
Being Black (dark) is Semantics in its every detail
Philosophizing the Nature of the Dark man - Wanting him to prevail

Let the Melanin that show through your darkest night
Be the hope you carry with your brightest light

Egypt is a Greek word - The meaning is Black (dark)
Arabs invaded Egypt
Rome invaded Egypt
Connotatively speaking - The Arabs have no more connection to Ancient Egypt
Than Europeans have to Ancient America - The truth is what I'm speaking
Mixed with invading Greeks – Persians – Romans –

46

Turks – Arabs - Libyans and
Europeans
Black Egyptians Natural Language had to change into another being
Being not what it was but what it is and what we are seeing
Even the layman's Linguist can decipher the truth to my meanings
Languages changing - Learning new dialects with every mix
Creating dilemmas for the masses
Trying to delete the Dark race with every fix
Fixating on the Anthropologist - Historians etc. that erases the truth
The Black man's proof
Knowing the truth, that even you can't deny
You slash the nose and slant the eye
Linguistically speaking, "Stop the Lie"
Dark Skin Color was here before Noah and Eli
Presently English is what I am speaking
My Israeli Language is what I'm seeking
My Dark skin I cherish and I'm keeping
My Black title is what I'm leaking (escaping)

WHAT IS IT ALL ABOUT?

They told the Khazars they were White/Caucasian
They told the Israelites/Judah they were Black/African American
persuasion
Our minds - A powerful tool
They created impeccable lies for all to be a fool

...

So we live our lives thinking it's all about skin color
While they are busy counting and spending our dollars
Words were taken out of the Bible and twisted to treat dark
people like trash
Scriptures misused to turn slavery into cash

...

Having another human laugh while another is hung and burnt
How about being on the other end - That will be a good lesson learnt
The White man is not our enemy but put in place for the plan
The plan of Satan to control every man
How can a White man be dominant over you
He could not speak your language - Doesn't that make him dumb too

...

He could not carry your load or endure your pain
He could not be taken from his family for it would send him insane
Only our Heavenly Father has power over you
Trust in him in all you do

...

For Satan has reign over the earth as we speak
He searches for the timid and destroy the weak
He control the minds of whomever will let him
He promise them riches for their soul
Their minds and body he takes control

...

There are Whites that truly want the truth to be told
But when they open their mouths their life is sold
For a price that they have to pay, so they nod and wink and
humbly obey

DON'T SPEND YOUR LIFE BEING A COLOR

It's all a part of controlling our neurological network. If we constantly see negative statements and images when it refers to what was given as our race (Black); our neurological network gets conditioned to that thought pattern and reacts to its learned definition. This is why it is extremely important to reorganize your neurological network with the positive truths. Don't let these definitions describe you. Don't even let these definitions alarm you. For in their subliminal treachery they deceive themselves. Not knowing our true soul will one day defend itself. Be honored by your dark skin tone but don't be defined by the Color (Black) they say is our race.

Definition of Black as quoted by: Second College Edition of The American Heritage Dictionary (Copyright 1982, 1985 by Houghton Mifflin Company - Boston)
"black (blak) adj. -er, -est. 1. Being of the darkest achromatic visual value; producing or reflecting comparatively little light and having no predominant hue.
2. Having little or no light: a black, moonless night. 3. Often Black. Belonging to an ethnic group having dark skin, esp. Negroid. 4. Dark in color: a face black with anger. 5. Soiled, as from soot; dirty. 6. Evil; wicked: black deeds. 7. Cheerless and depressing; gloomy: black thoughts. 8. Marked by anger or sullenness: gave him a black look. 9. Often Black. Attended with disaster; calamitous: the stock-market crash on Black Friday. 10. Deserving of, indicating, or incurring censure or dishonor: "man...has written one of his blackest records as a destroyer on the oceanic islands" (Rachel Carson)..."

Definition of White as quoted by: Second College Edition of The American Heritage Dictionary (Copyright 1982, 1985 by Houghton Mifflin Company - Boston)

"white (hwit, wit) adj. Whiter, whitest. 1. Being of the color white; devoid of hue, as new snow. 2. Approaching the color white; as: a. Pale; weaky colored; almost colorless: white wine. b. Pale gray; silvery and lustrous: white hair. c. Bloodless; blanched. 3. Light or whitish in color or having light of whitish parts. Used with animal and plant names; 4. a. Having the comparatively pale complexion typical of Caucasoids. b. Of, pertaining to, characteristic of, or dominated by Caucasians.

c. Slang. Fair or generous; decent: That was very white of you! 5. Not written or printed upon; blank. 6. Unsullied; pure. 7. Habited in white: white nuns. 8. Accompanied by or mantled with snow: a white Christmas. 9. a. Incandescent: white flames. b. Intensely heated; impassioned: white with fury. 10. Ultraconservative or reactionary."

REDEFINE YOUR BEAUTY

Redefine your beauty and see what the natural you is trying to say
Stop letting the world piece you together – Don't be a Frankenstein

Weaves with glue, perms and relaxers destroy hair cell DNA
It depletes our identifying symbol
Our race, our face, our heredity trace
The true you the evil one want to replace

The toxins in colors and perms may lead to cancer throughout the body
Then we will be nobody's hottie
Try henna colors - If you must color your hair

Redefine what they told you is beauty and you will see you
Creative - Distinctively explicit and wonderfully new

Be independent from years of servitude
No more social norms - Release them with gratitude

Grateful because you have become the real you
If we all do this our essence will shine globally through

Everywhere they look the essence of Judah beauty
His locks - Her curls - Thick and soft
It's easier than you think to shake the perms and straighteners off

Self-recovery is our goal
Releasing our cover-ups and freeing our soul

Letting others see what beauty is all about
Without even opening our mouth

Redefine your beauty because it's all you
I have saved thousands and you can too

YOU MUST BE CRAZY

You must be crazy if you think I'm going to give up my weave
You must be crazy if you think I'm going to let them see my naps
You think I'm walking around with this African looking crap
...
Now how does that sound about the beauty that's your hair
Strong and firm, nothing can compare
Braid It, dread it, afro it all around
Twist and curls and it's still your beautiful crown
Short, medium or long and flowing
It's all you that you should be showing
Your naps are not naps, you just need some control
A natural silky smooth shampoo and conditioner will soften it well
It will free the kinks and release the spells
...
You must be crazy - I love my perms
It makes my man love me and it makes heads turn
Weren't you the one who said he cheated on you
With your best friend and she has glued on hair too
It will make them look, it will make heads turn
But from the true self - A real man will never run
Run to your best friend - Nor the beauty on the side
He will walk beside you with love and pride
...
I must look like the video girls – I want to be a movie star
I want men with nice houses and a pimped out car
With the White women I have to compete
Not knowing it's yourself you delete
Straight hair and weaves are in
I don't want anyone to see me in my real condition

Keep the glory of self - In all you do
Real beauty has nothing to hide
No chemicals, no weaves, not even peroxide
No - I'm not crazy
I want you to adore the real you
Mind - Body and Soul that's true

WHAT'S UP WITH HER HAIR

What's up with her hair
It's curly and natural now
...

Wasn't it straight and long just two months ago
Wasn't it almost down to the floor
...

No - I think it was down near her back
Maybe she just took out their weaves and their tracks
...

What's up with her hair
It's more beautiful than before
What was she hiding and covering it for
...

What's up with her hair
Wow - It makes her beauty shine
Natural and curly
Soft and divine
...

What's up with her hair
I didn't know she had it like that
She looks like a princess or queen perhaps
With looks like hers
She should be on maps
...

A beauty as never before
Her hair - She now adore
Her smile shines truly
She has released her inner beauty
Wow! My love, you are the real cutie

Check out the cover photo with my all natural curly hair. I just love it! I went all natural several months ago. I had long hair that was all permed. I thought it was going to be a hard adjustment but after the first month, I was like "wow" I love my natural hair.

CHAPTER 4
SPIRITUAL CONNECTIONS

HIS GRACE

There were times when I thought that I was alone and without hope
With so many worries and struggles
Trying to cope

...

Moving from place to place
No friends around
No love for me - No one to be found

...

Educated and kind
Still they left me behind
I kept my sanity and held on to my mind

...

No opening at any place
No job to be found
So I fell to the ground
Not knowing what to do
Mortgage needed to be paid
I fell to my knees
Cried and prayed

...

Remembering His grace
He never left me
Those were trials you see
There was always shelter to keep me warm
His love and grace protecting me from harm

...

I received the message during my troubled times
It humbled my soul and freed my mind
His Grace - He has for me

His mercy so dear
His love so clear
In everything
Our Heavenly Father is always near

THERE MUST BE A WAY

There must be a way
For I don't want to give up the honeys
I don't want the guys to stop dishing me money

There must be a way
For me to win in my sin
To have it all and still drink gin

There must be a way
For me to have it all and still get to heaven
To do my dirt and play the number seven

There must be a way and then came you
Telling me to flee before the world is through

Why can't I win in my sin and continue to do my dirt
I pay my taxes and always work

You say flee from my sin and seek righteousness and peace
You say trust in our Heavenly Father and my temptations will stop

You say if I repent it will bring me closer to our Heavenly Father
If I do good and not sin it will bring him closer to me
Closer and dear as never before
Freeing the honeys and stopping the dirt
Cleansing my soul and uplifting my worth
Sobering me up to think clear all the time
Taking away my need for gin and wine

There must be a way
For this sin don't sound good anymore
I choose our Heavenly Father and his Heavenly shore

WHY IS IT SO HARD

Why is it so hard to admit that you were wrong
That you stumbled and fell and don't belong
...

Why is it so hard to see that you need his love
His truth and his guidance from up above
...

Why is it so hard to understand the sins of our fathers
Worshiping idols and praying to stones
Forgetting our Creator and cursing his throne
Why is it so hard to see that your sins keep you lost
Decorating trees and singing to Jack Frost
...

Eating from their tables and cleaning their stables
Falling into their every trap
...

Why is it so hard to understand why you must come out
Out from the plot, the lot, the tree and the frost
The sin that will cost you your very soul
Those things that will take you deep into the hole
...

Why is it so hard that you don't want to see
That it is from sin that you must flee

WHEN TIMES ARE HARD

When times are hard and you don't know what to do
Call on our Heavenly Father and Pray

Life is getting you down
Not one friend to be found
So much family but no one to trust
Knowing many but not really knowing much

When times are hard
Seek that quiet time and you will hear his voice
Feel his touch within your soul
For he gives us all a choice

No-where to turn
No-where to run
When life comes at you hard
No Visa - No Debit - No Master Card
Your life - It just seems marred
Your finances are week
Your bills they speak
But you don't know how to respond

When times are hard you need him the most
That is when he holds you close
He is your love and devoted partner
All you have to do is call
Sincere your will
Your mind - Keep still

Send your prayers to the one
Who has forgiven your sins
For he gave us his Son

VITAL FORCE

The vital force of my connection with this world
Takes me on a journey
Releasing powers unknown
Delivering wisdom
I've grown

Requiring no electrical power
To generate its birth
Vitality uncut
No disturbance of any kind
Forces of spirituality flowing through my mind

Vital Force and its strength
Leaping all bounds
That no super hero on earth has ever found

Powers from heaven
Not light years away
Visits my soul everyday

Energy traveling from on high
Tranquility measures and pleasures my soul
Peace within - The force control
The key to it all our Heavenly Father holds

<u>CELIBACY</u>

Focused on my purpose - My celibacy remains
With my true identity - My life proclaims
Divine in its glory
No need to explain
The true meaning of its spiritual gain

With peace and contentment
Spiritual delight
Joy and gladness always in sight
Praising my Heavenly Father for his greatness
For patience I have received
In his Holy word I believe
Only his trueness can conceive

My inner being expresses it well
Growth and empowerment from every cell
Loyalty to the Creator
His spirit always nearby
His wonders throughout Heaven
My soul comply

Celibacy in spirit – Truth - Justice and might
Focused on the most High
With every flight
I celebrate my celibacy
Holding on every step of the way
No pressure, no rush, nothing can persuade
My brain is clear - My energy remains
Understanding that's bold
My Heavenly Father's word spiritually told

Moral development that's pure
Health and life his cure
Within my celibacy I will endure

<u>WONDERFUL</u>

What greatness You hold
When You let your beauty be told

From the garden in which it began
You created a world so perfect and pure
Then You gave it to be cared for by man

Wonderful Your forgiveness of man's first sin
Your mercy - Your greatness released
Although without thought
In sin they were caught
With lessons they must be taught

Wonderful You are
You were never far
You watched over them throughout time
You showed them Your love
A covenant from above
Wonderful and divine

((((STILL THINKING ABOUT MARCUS))))

There was so many signs showing that he was wrong for me. Why did I pass them by? He was totally the opposite of me, but I guess I was one of those people who believed that opposites attract. Now looking at the situation... Before I met Marcus; I was such a Bible girl. I use to stay up all night reading my bible and watching Israelite videos. I love doing that but it irritated Marcus. I feel so taken. I missed out on so much. I cheated on my spirituality thinking that void that I was looking for was in a man when it was within me the entire time.

How could I let him lead me astray so easily?

I never...

I never...

He wanted to do that, not me.

He wanted to have control over me.

Why do we lose ourselves so easily?

How can I be assured that this won't happen again?

I was never taught as a child the powers that another can have over another—false power. The type of energy that drains the very soul—using words and giving broken promises—using touch and invoking spirits that take hold while changing direction—confusion all around—leading souls astray—bringing spirits together not equally yoked—stealing and not revealing the antidote.

We must learn to respect our soul. We must ask ourselves: What is my destiny? What is my purpose? What is the will of our Heavenly Father for me?

We give up on ourselves so easily. We meet a stranger and live out their dream or destiny. We bring purpose to their life while losing our own purpose and straying away from the will of our Heavenly Father. No man should have control over another.

WHY MUST YOU CONTROL ME

Why must you control me
You don't even know me
Is what I must say
...
You chose your mate because of her weakness
She chose you because of her meekness
You say you lost your job and now your rent is overdue
You slap your mate and forbid her to say it's over
If you knew who you were
You'd know it's a sin to slap her
To even raise your hand in anger brings your soul towards danger
With troubles you don't even want to unfold
Know thy-self, Love thy-self
Let your identity be unfold
...
Why must you control me
When you don't even know me
You want to be high and mighty
At the top of the world
Controlling all around you
But your voice was never heard
...
Heard the way you want it
Trying to control everything in sight
Bullying those who fear you
Doing everything except for right
The penalty will come for all that you have done

Long suffering at best - For your soul can't rest
You think you can win
You seek earthly gain and control
Check-mate - Your life is unfold

Why must you control me
When you can't control yourself
Learn who you are before your soul goes to rest

THE CURE

I am getting well naturally as you can see
Triumph over pain
Truth over rain

...

I've worked at the art of understand myself
Not being dependent
Knowing my worth
It is clear now
With spiritual knowledge, Wow

...

I use to ask, why
Why me
You are the chosen one
Can't you see
You have a higher place in this world – Here with me

...

You must be all that you can be
You can relate to the joys - Sufferings and pain
This makes you a great soul
A soul that can understand
Guide and lend a helping hand
Life that's unique
Compared to no other man

...

No more crying in despair
I know that my Heavenly Father is always near
No more worry about the past
The future is not yet
Knowing that my Heavenly Father has always been the cure
His love and protection is mine for sure

((((FLASH BACK – AT HOME WITH MOM))))

Mother - India are you talking to yourself again?

India - (Embarrassed) No ma, I'm getting ready for school.

Mother - Well hurry up young lady! I guess there is nothing wrong with you talking to yourself, just don't answer yourself back. "Don't forget to eat your breakfast!"

India - Wow ma! You made a feast this early?

{My mother smiles}

My mother was such an amazing cook. She knew how to throw it down in the kitchen. She did not just cook; she always ensured that our meals were nutritious. She was the best baker also. Her biscuits, cakes and pies were delicious. The taste just made you feel like you were in paradise. She always made sure we had the best when it came to food. She never cut corners.

Health

Health can be defined as a state of mental-
Social and physical well-being
What you are putting in your body is what I am freeing

...

Did you know that fresh basil tea will ease your anxiety
It's been said to set the mind free
Boil fresh parsley in water to make tea
It will cleanse your system and take out what's old
Freshly chopped ginger boiled in water
Will soothe a sore throat and comfort your cold
Not only will it assist in lowering blood pressure
It is well known as a cholesterol blesser

...

The lesser will be known
If we fail to attend to the needs of the mind, body and soul
Feed your mind with knowledge and nutrients
It heals neurons and cells

...

Generate your body with nutritious foods
Herbs that make it thrive with vitality
Sooth your soul with the spiritual truths
Spiritual truths bring the Bible to reality

...

Think health while doing your daily activities
Your decisions will surprise you

...

That my friend will release something that you never knew
Think health my friend and Heavenly too

(((LATER THAT DAY AT SCHOOL)))

Travis was so cool. He always looked after me. Who is Travis? Travis was someone I could talk to about anything as a child. He was my best male friend. He was also my first Crush.

Travis - India, India!

Travis - Wow girl, you were day dreaming for a while. Aren't you going to sit down?

India – Travis have you ever wondered…. Don't you want to get away from it all? Things are changing. It's like I see a store front church and liquor store on almost every corner. Our neighbors are not like family any more. Everyone seems to have a problem with each other now. What is going on? We use to keep the doors to our home unlocked during the day.

No more of that because:

THEIR POCKETS GETTING FATTER

Their pockets getting fatter
So what's the matter
Standing on the corner shooting dice
Late in the evening sipping whiskey
No ice
Waiting for the junkie to pass you by
Ten bucks, twenty – For the next fix or high
Cruising down the road in your Chevy Impala
Waiting for the girls to say twenty or fifty dollars
Picking up strangers all in the night
Not thinking about your health or your life

...

Going to church on Sunday
"Well, I paid my tithes"
At the bus stop while the Preacher Drives by in his custom Buick
LeSabre
How much money did you savor

...

Their pockets getting fatter
So what's the matter

...

Rent is due
All your money is gone
He has a mansion
Where is your home

...

Your Screen door is busted
The window has many cracks
Stop fluffing their pockets
Stop filling their sacks
Our Messiah was a Carpenter
What is your trade
Don't be no one's Nigger or Slave
Their pockets getting fatter and that is the subject matter

PENCIL ART BY DANTE' WILSON

(((CONTINUATION OF: LATER THAT DAY AT SCHOOL)))

Travis - India, the Instructor is coming—Shhhhhhhhhhhhhh!

India - I'm tired of reading about the lies and writing essays about Christopher Columbus. Christopher Columbus didn't discover America! Why are we always learning these lies?

It was my turn to read my report/essay and this is what they got:

THEY CREATED A LIE – TO MAKE US FRY

They told a lie
To make us fry
To burn our souls in hell
We thought it was cool to do drugs
We thought it was cool to rob - Cheat and steal
We thought it was cool to take what was not ours
We thought it was cool to stay forever high (drugged out)
Not knowing it would take us to the slave plantation - Not Heaven
You made a lie
To make us fry
You said education will get you far
I have a Doctors Degree and no job
My fancy loans are way overdue
The lies you told are not coming true
They created a lie
To make us fry
The American dream is what they promised
Holding signs under bridges while wiping down cars
He fought for his country; we should lift him higher
Lost and alone, no job, no retire
They created a lie
To make us fry
...

You said show a little skin, if you want to get the man
You forgot to tell us - It was not in the Creator's plan
I showed the skin and got the man
In the morning he's Steve and at night he's Fran
You created a lie
To make us fry

...

You said take one sniff - It will take all of your worries away
Now I am hooked and my brain is gone astray
No worries - No nothing - No more the same me
It took my family - My friends - I don't recognize what I see
They created a lie
To make us fry

I WAS A BIG HIT WITH MY CLASS-MATES BUT A BUST WITH THE INSTRUCTOR.

Instructor - "Go to the principal's office, now!"

(Students started talking loud and commenting on my poem.)

Instructor - Settle down now! India, go to the principal's office now young lady.

I'm not going to lie; I was afraid to go to the Principles office. Why? Well it was my 3rd time this month. I knew exactly what he was going to say. He is always getting on my case. I just don't get it? I am an Honor student, so why won't they let me speak my mind like Malcolm X?

(I entered Principal Brown's office as the bell rang for my next class.)

India - Hello Principle Brown!

Principal – India, I just received a call concerning a poem you read a few minutes ago and...

(I cut him off)

India - Principal Brown, must I apologize?

Principal - Let me see the poem. (Laughter: Ha, ha, ha, ha) Apologize for what? Telling the truth! Beautiful poem but how many times must I tell you that there is a time and place for everything? That wasn't the time and especially in Mr. Trumbal's class! I will talk to Mr. Trumbal. Remember: There is a time and place for everything.

Principal – Take this pass and go to your next class.

India – Thank you!

(Principal Brown gave me this look as if he knew I was going to do the right thing—He smiled at me and shook his head. Yes, a time and place for everything—I always kept those words with me. They helped me to stop and think before acting). **"Most of the time"**

JUST LOOK

Just look and you will see - That there is more to this reality
People, places
Trading different spaces
Coming, going and never really knowing

...

OK! What is it all for
A master plan already set
A mega plan that we haven't figured out yet
Over and over life is repeated
Reliving confusion
Trying to figure out dilution

...

Hoping the good turn into great
Maybe it's about the family
Let's create

...

Slow down and rest a while
For you have walked so many miles

...

Stop to smell the roses
Look before it closes
There is something trying to get your attention
Feel the spirit and start to listen
Oh the peace must be mention

...

In my corner you will find
A loving home and peace of mind
Just look and you will see
The Heavenly Father in you
The Heavenly Father in me

(((BACK TO MARCUS)))

(Door Bell: DING DONG)

India - huh, Who could that be?

(DING DONG)

Marcus - India, it's me .

India - The door is open!

Marcus - Hey what's up? Don't worry I won't be in your way, I'm just here to get the rest of my things. Hey India.

India - What?

Marcus – You look a mess. Don't let the breakup get to you.

India - You look a hot mess too. Just get your things and go!

As I watch him struggling to carry his things out, All I could think about was goals I should have accomplished. I could have finished my book by now. Instead, I settled for someone that was playing me. I should have waited for someone who would have appreciated me. I know; you don't have to tell me twice. Should have, could have, would have but didn't.

MISTAKE

A mistake is said to be an error or fault
I thought I had knowledge
Wasn't I taught

...

Did I have a weakness not known to me
Was it his lies that I did not see
Was I responsible for all that I endured
Did I not know that I could be cured

...

Cured from his torture and misery
They say no pain
No gain
What kind of relief is this
With this mistake I shall truly reign
For it has cost me almost everything

...

I must be watchful in my future encounters
For I trust to easy
Error and Pain
Peace I will claim
Understanding that this is no game

I KNOW THERE IS SOMEONE OUT THERE WHO WILL LOVE ME THE
RIGHT WAY. I'M NOT GOING TO BLAME EVERY MAN FOR WHAT ONE MAN
DID TO ME. I'M TOO STRONG FOR THAT. I MUST HAVE FAITH!

BROTHERS & SISTERS

Remember the day when all they could do was jump over a broom
Our ancestors were not allowed to have a honeymoon
Remember the day when our ancestors were sold
Working hard in the fields in minus degree cold
Not allowed to be with their men
While being forced to live in sin

...

Black man - Know that you are our king
Black women know that you are the reigning queen

...

Humble yourself and be there for your man
Black man - Respect her mothering and understand

...

Don't argue because he lost his job
Encourage him with love and let him know sometimes are hard
But don't give into the struggles in your day
Don't throw your troubles in each other's face
Take out the garbage and keep your own house clean
Be the man and women that our ancestors were seeing

...

Seeing in the past as they worked in the fields
Taking whips and chains across their backs without any shields
They knew it would be better for the families to come
Lift up each other for our struggles are one

...

When you learn your true identity
You will know that you were never meant to be each other's enemy
Respect the Judah man and lift him up
Respect the Judah woman and lift her up
Remember our race is in the Creator's cup

Bless my Heavenly Father for my soul. I am getting back to the spiritual me. There is no time for me to slack.

THE SLACKER

The slacker indeed
I must proceed
Why put off for tomorrow what you can do today
Learn who you are so your true self you can portray

...

So you don't like reading the Bible
You go to church instead
Are you really sure it's truth that they are putting in your head

...

Don't be a slacker
Study for yourself
You heard the saying
Knowledge is power
Be a believer
It's near our final hour

...

I went to school
I worked hard all day
Is that all you have
Will that be the last words you'll say

...

You read books telling you about the moon
You write stories that turn life into a cartoon

...

You have time for things that bring you no peace
If you have all you ever wanted
Would your anger then cease

...

The Slacker results turn into a hacker living life that is not his or
her own
Do your research
Learn about yourself
Our Messiah
Our truth
Our thrown

Time has passed since my break-up with Marcus. I'm starting to feel the side effects of loneliness. I'm in a crowd but I still feel lonely. Why do I feel so sad? Everything is happening so fast. I was supposed to be happily married. I know that I am truly blessed. My basic needs are happily met. I have travel throughout the oceans shores and even served our country in the military. Awards I've won but attention near none. I know I'm dreaming right now, but dreams do come true. So...I can't let sadness get me down. I can't and I won't!

I need spiritual peace in my life. These past few weeks have been so hectic. I need to know about love and the true meaning of it. I need to release this confusion that has come over me; A confusion that is trying to out shine my blessings.

AMAZING GRACE

Spiritual challenges throughout the day
Guiding me and clearing my way
Remarkable is the truth that I see
Blessing my soul tremendously

...

Amazing Grace that surrounds my space
Replacing negative traces in every case

...

Collecting from the Divine
Knowledge and truth with every sign
Enlightening my mind
While cleansing me from sin
Taking me into places that I have never been

...

Amazing Grace comforts my soul
Uplifts my spirits and taking control

...

Amazing grace he has for me
Throughout my life and eternity

<u>PEACE</u>

Someone told me that there will never be peace in this world of ours
With bombs, guns and nuclear powers

...

Is it harmony you want
With all getting along
No more wars and nothing going wrong

...

We don't think about this deep enough because we continue in
our sins
For the return for that
No one wins

...

We must look a lot higher
We must trust in the Messiah

...

Come out of her and flee
For her sins have no degree
For it is peace you must see

...

His words we must follow
The Bible was never hollow
Its words filled through and through

...

The sinful way is not the road to travel
A dead-end you will find

...

Peace comes in only one form
From our Heavenly Father who protects from the storm

...

If it's peace you want
Leave sin behind
Flee from the treachery of sin
Seek "Peace"
It's Divine

<u>SPIRITUAL</u>

More intimate – My relationship
Inspired by his personal touch

Loving power surrounds me
Revealing not less but much

In sync with his vibrations
My inspiration flows

Touching the deepest water
As my knowledge spiritually grows

Spiritual - Not organized religion
Personal relationship with my Heavenly Father

No ritual or burning candles to a deity without breath
No taking bribes to increase an outer wealth

Serving with free will
Heavenly blessings - My cup he fill

Introspective thoughts to the Creator
Dwelling on his every word without having to try

Spiritual - Yes
In our Heavenly Father – We all are blessed

SILENCE

In the still of the night
Sounds of nature reveal
Their life - Their story and noises so real

Listen with your mind
Not a sound to be heard
Listen a little closer
And he will reveal his words

Words of enlightenment
Directions to your path
Wisdom in moments
No worries of his wrath

Silence yourself and find your peace within
You always had the strength
You are powerful in him

Control the weakness that let others take over you
Silence my dear - His strength lives in you too

Fear has no place for the soul that is bold
Silently carrying our Heavenly Father's force
Taking you through life and its spiritual course

In the silence of every moment that you hold so dear
Listen with pureness - It reveals itself so clear

Today I'm feeling so much better...

FORGIVE ME

FORGIVE ME
When I woke up this morning and did not thank you for another day
For going straight to bed and forgetting to pray

FORGIVE ME
For yelling - When I could have lowered my tone
For being angry because of the other persons moan

FORGIVE ME
For not smiling - When I knew it could have made someone else's day
Knowing he was lost and not showing him the way

FORGIVE ME
When I took two and all I needed was one
For being impatient when all I had was time
For thinking about only what's on my mind

FORGIVE ME
For rushing and trying to hurry the bible through
For not slowing down and teaching others the truth

FORGIVE ME
For taking my time when it comes to you
For not putting you first in all I do

FORGIVE ME
For saying things I know I shouldn't say
For acting in not the holiest way

Forgive me Heavenly Father and show me the righteous way
Help me to live holy with love and peace portray
I will continue to praise you every day

I have to start reading the bible more. I have put too much focus on someone who never knew me and never truly cared about me. I must put all of my focus on my Heavenly Father. He knows me better than I know myself.

THE BIBLE AND ALL ITS WISDOM

Read the Bible
You will obtain wisdom
Knowledge as never before
No teacher can teach
No preacher can preach
What only you and you alone need to decipher
From the beginning to the end he laid out the plan
For all mankind to explore
The teacher teaches what he wants you to learn
The preacher preaches what he wants to earn
In it most of them want personal gain
If you read it yourself you'll understand
All of the life lessons it contain
Don't blow it off
Like a novel - Fact or fiction
It's not a love story for your personal addiction
No action that takes you to the moon
No horror to keep you up in the night
No week-end or midnight fright
What you will find is an exceptional book
It will guide you - Inspire you and open up a brand new world
It will teach you about our Heavenly Father
His creations - Spiritual path and revelation

It will take you to a place that your soul desire
It will take your mind and body higher
For your personal relationship with him you will learn
That no religion can control
Your spiritual wealth you will earn
The truth he will unfold
It's your map to salvation - Your course is throughout
You can start at the beginning or end
For the strength lies in your hand
For your spirit will guide you and release its mysteries
It will help you understand
No fiction you will find
Just transliterations
Done by man
So you would not understand the Creator's plan
So only the elite will know
So they can obtain wealth and power
So only their class can grow

Not our Heavenly Father's plan
To mislead you by using different names
You must continue to read it just the same
For extreme knowledge you will gain

Transliterations and changing of names
Does not take away from his word
For stories are repeated
And his guidance throughout
Teaching our Heavenly Father's will
How to live
With commandments all about
Instructions on what to call him
Instructions on what not to call him

Telling us who the deceiver is
How the deceiver will rise and how the deceiver will fall
The stories throughout the bible is for all
For all to know
For all to grow
Obtain wisdom - Spiritual wealth and knowledge

So when the chips are down
No one around
And life appears to be hard to control
People everywhere giving you strife
Feeling lost and alone
Mother crying
Children dying
Drugs all over the streets
Jobs firing - People spying
No one around you can trust
Pockets empty - Gas tank low
Not very far you can go
Read the Bible an answer you will find
With it keep an open mind
Read with heart and soul
Treasure it as much as gold
Transliterations were abused
So that you will refuse to use and read this remarkable creation
To deceive you with hate and make you debate
And go against our Heavenly Father's will
But in it the truth remains

EXPRESSIONS

Words cannot express the love I feel when I wake up in the morning
Just knowing that someone love me
So much that my presence is alive another day
Just knowing that he has already created my way

Someone so great - So marvelous has time for me
Clearing the way and making life easier to see

Expressions of love to the highest degree
For the mercy he has shown me when times were rough
To feel his love in my every being
Seeing and knowing it is from sin that I am fleeing

Expressing desires of being holy
Cleaning my soul and walking boldly
Feeling love so dear
Nothing on earth will ever compare

No mountain to high
No valley to low
For his greatness will forever show
Expressing the joy that electrifies every cell
That gives me strength and keeps me living well

My Heavenly Father is all there ever was
Searching no more to fill an empty space
I am his child - I keep his grace
While expressions leave me with love tender and warm
His protection as he carries me in his arm

JOY

When I think of our Heavenly Father's greatness - I feel joy
The greatness of his power flows throughout my soul
Happiness on every level in my life - It has its role

I delight in my everyday routine
I keep my environment peaceful and serene
The joy that he has given me unfolds on every scene

Unspeakable joy when times are distress
Silently fills my soul
As my heart beats slowly
Our Heavenly Father's presence acts boldly to protect me from all harm
The joy that his spirit sends me heals all wounds in life with charm

Joy - Unspeakable joy - A treasure within itself
Silent whispers - Soft touch - Gentle feelings from within
The joy that our Creator gives is pure and without sin

Joy – Joy - Joy
Happiness in spirit
Wonderfully portrayed
Worshiping my Heavenly Father as I sing and pray
For his everlasting Joy - In my heart it shall stay

COUNT YOUR BLESSINGS

Count your blessings and not the times you couldn't pay your bills
Count your blessings and not the doctor prescribed pills
Count your blessings and not the times they made you cry
Count your blessings and stop always asking why

Count your blessings and not the pimples on your face
Count your blessings and stop wanting what others have
Count your blessings and leave your jealousy at the door
Count your blessings because he could have made you poor

Count your blessings stop depending on another's will
Count your blessings you could have been born still

Count your blessings because there is only one you
Count your blessings you are treasured and precious too

Count your blessings he smiles when you are true
Count your blessings remember it's all up to you

Count your blessings you are one of his chosen
Count your blessings for your life has just begun

Count your blessings for his hands stretches out to you
Count your blessings for he loves you in spite of what you do

Count your blessings for there is none like our Heavenly Father
Count your blessings for he's the one that will take you higher

Count your blessings and see what our Heavenly Father has done
He woke you up this morning - Started you on your way - Fed you

Clothe you and gave you a place to stay
Count your blessings and let your beautiful light shine
For you are a creation of our Heavenly Father - He will give you
peace of *mind*

It seems like everything was so much easier when I was younger...

REFLECTIONS

Moments never to be re-created
A past that stole the innocence of the young
Looking back reminiscing – How I laughed - Lived and learned
Remembering an astonishing discovery
Changing my thoughts of young gifted and black

...

Roots on television
No previous lessons on racism
Slavery never mentioned in my home
Not knowing my heritage was mistreated
Not knowing their plan was not completed
To delete the trace upon our face
To abuse the men within our race

...

Traces of the past within the deep parts of my soul
Slowly resurfacing
Slowly discovering my royal role
It's my time to know
Unmasking the lie

...

The lie that keep my people down and out in the inner cities
Not knowing or believing in their worth
Fathers leaving mothers
No man to strengthen his birth
Wanting and needing something to take away the pain
They brought drugs and alcohol to my people
To keep them contained

...

The ultimate truth I must reveal
Reflecting within my soul
My people I must help heal

(((More drama with Marcus)))

(I see him in the food court at the mall arguing with a woman, the woman slaps him)

Me being me, I walked up to them.

India – Hi Marcus, I thought you were going to Paris. Who is your friend?

Woman – I'm his wife Paris. Who are you?

India – I'm his ex-girlfriend. My name is India.

Marcus looked shocked and his face was red from the slap

India – Marcus broke up with me because he stated that he did not want to be in a relationship anymore and wanted to focus on his goals. He told me that he was moving to Paris. Wow! Your name is Paris. I guess the joke is on me. (I laugh: Ha, ha, ha and a tear falls from my eye.)

Woman – Marcus and I got married two weeks ago at city hall. So no, the joke is on me because I lost the baby that I was carrying for him and I just found out that Marcus lost his job.

Marcus – Paris, let's go!

Woman – Nice meeting you India, I am sorry about everything.

(Paris [Woman] walks away and Marcus walks behind her.)

I am thinking: "What just happened?" Breathe and relax...

I must not let this be a distraction and take me off course because Marcus's chapter has ended in my life. I must move on and let go. I must keep my happiness. I gave up my freedom once. No room in my thoughts for past issues.

I am free now but I can't believe Marcus lied to me. He must have thought that he would never see me again. The surprise of him being here was not as shocking as seeing him being slapped. He was such a bully when he was with me.

I must take control of my thoughts. I will not let this take away from my happiness!

KEEPING MY HAPPINESS

Sunshine - You sure look nice today
Sadness - I don't have time to play

I'm looking up and into the future
Past out
Cast out
It's a new day

Since the truth - My life has just begun
Say what
Pay cut
Try another son
Life has just begun

You are not the only one
Wait a minute
Hold your head up high hun
Happiness is creative fun

Are you trying to give yours away
I'm keeping my happiness
I don't have time for stress
No trash - No mess
Peace and Happiness

Shalom

It's time for me to complete my book but I need a break from all the drama. I need a vacation but...

NO TIME FOR REST

I am extremely tired
My back is sore
My feet are numb and I am sleepy for sure

...

Why can't I sleep
I have nothing on my mind
How much of this can I endure
Maybe there is something my Heavenly Father wants me to find

...

Walking through my home
I have done every chore
My bones are starting to ache down to the core
No time for rest comes to my mind
I picked up my Bible it was divine
The words I read - I understood for the first time

...

This time I am enlightened as never before
Wow! How splendid is the truth, it is my open door
My truth was here all the time because of the rumors before I
could not find
My eyes wide opened - I am a true Israelite
Counting my blessings all through the night
Since I am one of his chosen - I must help lead the way
For many of our people are lost and astray
No time for rest - There is work to be done
I am finally at peace
I am one with his son

CHAPTER 5
IDOL WORSHIP AND TRANSLITERATIONS

Now that I am back on the right path, I must not allow the controls of this world to manipulate me any further. No person, place or thing—No idols within my ring...

IDOL WORSHIP FOR SURE

Idol worship for sure
But there is a cure
It starts in the mind
Subliminal implant
Mass media sold
Multibillion dollar business
Already gold

...

Perception mislead
Corruption was fed
Transplant after transplant images living in our head
Believing in a force will cost you your soul
For the Creator clearly told
You shall have no other God before him

...

There is only one Creator
His spirit lives in us - For we are not greater
His spirit is our connection not idols
When you worship idols you place your energy in those beings
Creating evil that remain to be seen
Awakening evils that were cast out
Bringing your judgment clearly about

...

Everything has its purpose
A chair to sit in
A vase for a flower
Never bow to a man-made tower/throne or figurine
For his wrath is yet to be seen
Our Heavenly Father is the Creator

How dare you disrespect him
Praying to a picture, wood, plastic or gold
For in the days of Moses his warnings were clearly foretold
Don't think in our time that he has forgotten
For their wicked sins - They had to pick cotton
For your sins he will return
Give up the idols - Repent and learn

1 John 4:1, "Beloved, believe not every spirit, but try the spirits whether they are of God: because many false prophets are gone out into the world." Acts 17:24 God that made the world and all things therein, seeing that he is Lord of heaven and earth, dwelleth not in temples made with hands;

Acts 7:48 Howbeit the most High dwelleth not in temples made with hands; as saith the prophet, 49 Heaven is my throne, and earth is my footstool: what house will ye build me? saith the lord: or what is the place of my rest? 50 Hath not my hand made all these things?

IDOL WORSHIP
TRUTH OR LIE - LETS CONTEMPLATE

The famous picture that many blacks place on their walls; thinking that it is a picture of Jesus Christ is that of Cesare Borgia. Cesare Borgia posed for these and many other pictures that many of our Israel/Judah tribe pray to and pray in front of. Artists have also used the facial features of Cesare Borgia to create other images to portray Jesus Christ.

Cesare Borgia, alleged illegitimate son of Pope Alexander VI, modeled for numerous photos used to represent Jesus Christ. He was a Spanish-Italian cardinal that resigned his church office to become a military commander and leading figure in politics. Leonardo Di Vinci was alleged to have been commissioned by Pope Alexander VI to recast Jesus Christ in the image of his son Cesare Borgia with the intent of passing off historical Jesus as European in appearance.

Exodus 20:4 Thou shalt not make unto thee any graven image, or any likeness of any thing that is in heaven above, or that is in the earth beneath, or that is in the water under the earth: 5 Thou shalt not bow down thyself to them, nor serve them: for I the LORD thy God am a jealous God, visiting the iniquity of the fathers upon the children unto the third and fourth generation of them that hate me; 6 And showing mercy unto thousands of them that love me, and keep my commandments.

JESUS PORTRAITS AND NAME

Portraits and Name a constant debate
Truth or lie
Lets contemplate

They say his photo is just a symbol to relate to and
His name has no relation to Zeus

They say it's just a trick to throw us off
So that we get confused
So the name Jesus we won't use

It's a constant discussion we must get clear
For the end of time is drawing near

The name Jesus is said to be derived from Middle English
Then derived from Old English = Jesus
Then taken from late Latin = Iesu
Then taken from Greek = Iesous (translated to mean Hail Zeus)
Then taken from Hebrew

HEBREW LINGUISTICS

Constructed from the old
Designed into the new
Old Hebrew
Your voice remain
Your people contain
Variety in groups separated
Place to place
Dialects changing from race to race
Helping us to understand our beginning - We trace

PHOENICIAN ALPHABET

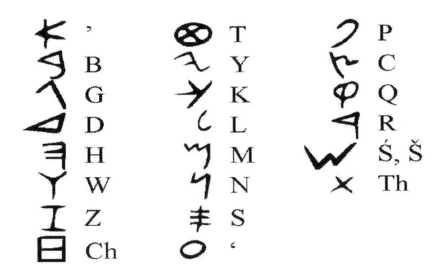

PHOENICIAN ALPHABET CHART

Letter	Name	Meaning	Transliteration	Corresponding letter in				
				Hebrew	Arabic	Greek	Latin	Cyrillic
𐤀 𝌆	'āleph	ox	'	א	ا	Aα	Aa	Аа
𐤁	bēth	house	b	ב	ٮ	Bβ	Bb	Бб, Вв
𐤂	gimel	camel	g	ג	ح	Γγ	Cc, Gg	Гг
𐤃	dāleth	door	d	ד	د	Δδ	Dd	Дд
𐤄	hē	window	h	ה	ه	Εε	Ee	Ее, Єє
𐤅	wāw	hook	w	ו	و	(Ϝϝ), Υυ	Ff, Uu, Vv, Ww, Yy	Уу
𐤆	zayin	weapon	z	ז	ز	Ζζ	Zz	Зз
𐤇	hēth	fence	ḥ	ח	ح	Ηη	Hh	Ии
𐤈	ṭēth	wheel	ṭ	ט	ط	Θθ		Ѳф
𐤉	yōdh	arm	y	י	ى	Ιι	Ii, Jj	Іі
𐤊	kaph	palm	k	כ	ك	Κκ	Kk	Кк
𐤋	lamedh	goad	l	ל	ل	Λλ	Ll	Лл

ϻ	ᛘ	mēm	water	m	מ	م	Μμ	Mm	Mм
ϟ	ϟ	nun	fish	n	נ	ن	Nν	Nn	Нн
‡	‡	sāmekh	fish	s	ס	س	Ξξ, Χχ	Xx	Xx
O	O	ʿayin	eye	ʿ	ע	ع	Oo	Oo	Oo
?	?	pē	mouth	p	פ	ف	Ππ	Pp	Пп
ⵔ	ⵔ	sādē	papyrus plant	s	צ	ص	ϻϡ		Цц, Чч
ϙ	ϙ	qōph	monkey	q	ק	ق	Ϙϙ	Qq	
◁	◁	rēš	head	r	ר	ر	Ρρ	Rr	Pp
W	W	šin	tooth	š	ש	ش	Σσ	Ss	Cc, Шш
X	+	tāw	mark	t	ת	ت	Ττ	Tt	Tr

PHOENICIAN ALPHABET
WIKIMEDIA COMMONS
Creative Commons Attribution Share-Alike 3.0 Unported

HEBREW ALPHABET

אבגדהוזחטיכךללםם

Mem Mem Lamed Khaf Khaf Yod Teit Cheit Zayin Vav He Dalet Gimel Beit Aleph

ננסעפפצצקרשת

Tav Shin Reish Qof Tzadi Tzadi Peh Peh Ayin Samekh Nun Nun

(PUBLIC DOMAIN)

PLATE I.—TABLE OF HEBREW AND CHALDEE LETTERS.

Number	Sound or Power	Hebrew and Chaldee Letters	Numerical Value	Roman character by which expressed in this work	Name	Signification of Name
1.	a (soft breathing).		1. (Thousands are	A.	Aleph.	Ox.
2.	b, bh (v).		2. denoted by a	B.	Beth.	House.
3.	g (hard), gh.		3. larger letter ;	G.	Gimel.	Camel.
4.	d, dh (flat th).		4. thus an Aleph	D.	Daleth.	Door.
5.	h (rough breathing).		5. larger than the	H.	He.	Window.
6.	v, u, o.		6. rest of the let-	V.	Vau.	Peg, nail.
7.	z, dz.		7. ters among	Z.	Zayin.	Weapon, sword.
8.	ch (guttural).		8. which it is,	Cн.	Cheth.	Enclosure, fence.
9.	t (strong).		9. signifies not 1,	T.	Teth.	Serpent.
10.	i, y (as in yes).		10. but 1000.)	I.	Yod.	Hand.
11.	k, kh.	Final = ך	20. Final = 500	K.	Caph.	Palm of the hand.
12.	l.		30.	L.	Lamed.	Ox-goad.
13.	m.	Final = ם	40. Final = 600	M.	Mem.	Water.
14.	n.	Final = ן	50. Final = 700	N.	Nun.	Fish.
15.	s.		60.	S.	Samekh.	Prop, support.
16.	O, aa, ng (gutt.).		70.	O.	Ayin.	Eye.
17.	p, ph.	Final = ף	80. Final = 800	P.	Pe.	Mouth.
18.	ts, tz, j.	Final = ץ	90. Final = 900	Tz.	Tzaddi.	Fishing-hook.
19.	q, qh (guttur.).		100. (The finals are not	Q.	Qoph.	Back of the head.
20.	r.		200. always considered	R.	Resh.	Head.
21.	sh, s.		300. as bearing an in-	Sн.	Shin.	Tooth.
22.	th, t.		400. creased numeri-cal value.)	Tн.	Tau.	Sign of the cross.

CHAPTER 6
THE LINGUISTIC JOURNEY

Former Names of Countries and Cities

Ethiopia = Abyssinia
Iran = Persia
Iraq = Mesopotamia

MAPPING OUT THE JOURNEY

Mapping out the journey from coast to coast
Yes - Sometimes life is hard
Traveling to and fro
Sometimes places you don't know
Meeting people without any being
No existence in their eyes
No smile to be seen
In their face no expression at all
All over the globe
Get up don't fall
Be strong my people
For we must understand
It's in the works and a part of the plan
Remember through it all serve no man

...

Our Heavenly Father is the Creator
Always and Forever
No Force - No course should ever lead you astray
For our Creator is our protector he will never decay

...

There should be no surprises in this journey
For the Bible maps it out
Their experience becomes our experience
In different times
From different minds
From generation to generation to come

...

When you hear of wars
It's been here before
When you see death
Know that our ancestors have left
When you see suffering and pain
Remember the story of Cain

...

Don't see your life as some big surprise and think - Oh - Why me
For this journey you must proceed and in the end you will see
So - Rediscover the land of your beginning
Your heritage - Your worth
See how far you have traveled
And where you have ended up on this earth
Their thoughts became your thoughts
For your actions don't stand alone
Map out your journey
Discover your home

If you every wonder why you are restless--Your soul misses its home...

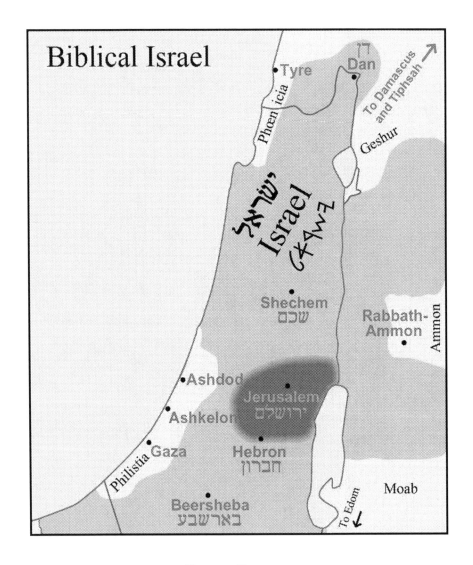

Biblical Israel

Tyre
Phœnicia
Dan
דן
To Damascus and Tiphsah
Geshur

ישראל
Israel
לארשי

Shechem
שכם

Rabbath-Ammon
Ammon

Ashdod
Jerusalem
ירושלם
Ashkelon
Philistia Gaza
Hebron
חברון
Moab
To Edom
Beersheba
בארשבע

KINGDOMS OF ISRAEL AND JUDAH MAP

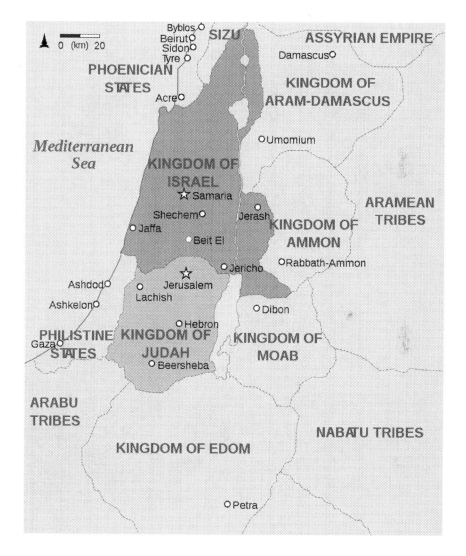

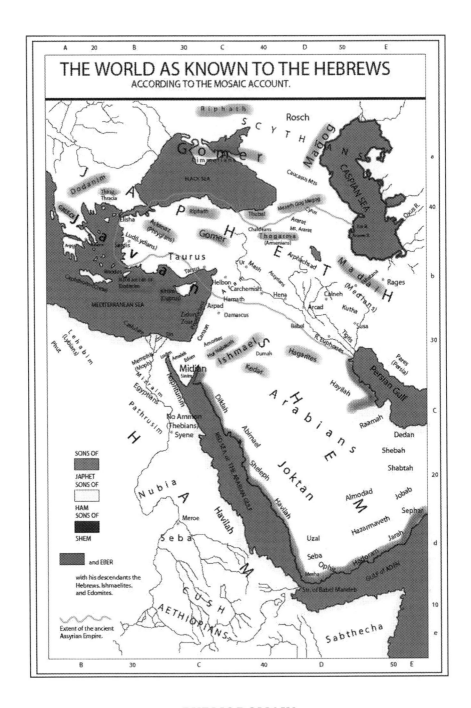

THE WORLD AS KNOWN TO THE HEBREWS

ACCORDING TO THE MOSAIC ACCOUNT.

PUBLIC DOMAIN

THE GORY IN GOREE

How skillfully planned was the transport of their journey
Face to Face
Place to Place

The name of this island says it all
For Gory was their story
No luxury cruise
Hurt and abused
Misled and misused
Oh how confused

No choice - Can't choose
Captured and forced to lose
But the story isn't over yet

**GOREE ISLAND, SENEGAL
PUBLIC DOMAIN**

Israel/Judah were taken to this island after being captured for transport on ships headed to Cuba, Brazil, and the United States for slavery.

INSIDE THE SLAVE HOUSE ON GOREE ISLAND, SENEGAL

PUBLIC DOMAIN

DESTINATION USA

Destination USA
Settled on these shores

...

Vessel
All on board

...

Population count many
Represented by each dot
Segregated and aggravated not owning any lots

...

The future is here
Dots slowly disappear
But there are still those we can count
It's not over until all dots are gone
When zero is the amount

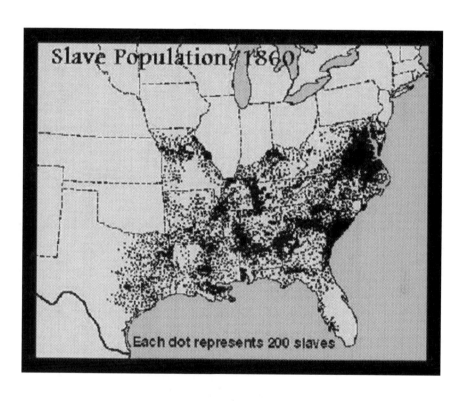

PUBLIC DOMAIN

THE WORLD'S POPULATION

The world's population has been estimated to reach
Approximately 7 billion 2012
They say that we are the minority in this population estimate
So we give up hope and think we can't win

...

If you calculate all of the Blacks and Africans throughout the world
We dominate - Destined to be prominent

...

We even grow in China - India and the United States
Highest Populated Countries although we are the minority
We are everywhere that's why annihilating us is their priority

...

They put us (The true Hebrews) against the Africans
They told us they sold our race into slavery
But we must remember - The greatest story that's ever told
Throughout the Bible we are unfold
That's why they try to discredit the Bible
For that they will be Liable

...

Why do you think Aids is rampant
To delete Blacks and Africans from this planet
Their creation of Aids is the trap that's set
Trying to say that we are all drug users - Sexual deviants is how
the trap is met

...

We live in this world and we are a major part of the population too
So why do we continually let others have control over our roots
Invading our Countries where we are the majority
Creating Laws and taking over authority
United we stand – They know that divided we fall
We must defeat those that have defeated us - For once and for all

REORGANIZE YOUR NEUROLOGICAL NETWORK

Your learned behavior and beliefs through training and education
Has influenced your neurological network

...

Reorganize your neurological network through self-actualization
Learn about your true heritage
Not of that in the European History Books
Research and retrace the tracks of your ancestors History
For in your studies you will see - that you were never a mystery

...

When you learn who you truly are - you reorganize your brain function
Creating new neurological paths for a natural process

...

Know your true culture - its values - goals and practices
Your intellect is longing for a higher degree of itself to be known
Promote your being - let it shine from your thrown
When you develop your intellect through self-knowledge
you develop personal quality

...

Whether analytical, competent, cooperative, honest or courageous
Your personal quality will release powers
That are true Israelites and Heavenly contagious

...

Royal in statue
Laced in gold, myrrh and incense
Remembering the covenant with Adam and the Word that was sent
Follow this story down the Nile with its essence
From Ethiopia thru the trails of the Sudan
Our beginning and that of man

HELP IS ON THE WAY

I was standing in line awaiting my turn
When this old gentleman asked was my skin sunburned
I told him no - I was beautifully born this way
He replied with - What a wonderful thing to say

...

He told me that I looked just like his mother
My nose, my head, my every feature
He kept starring and said, "You are such a lovely creature."
I thought, what a strange thing to say
He went on and said, "Don't be dismayed."

...

He asked where I was from and I told him where I was born
He said no not there - Your heritage - Your throne
So I talked about my great-great grandmother's home

...

He said, "I know your people--We are cousins for sure."
You are my family that they took
You disappeared from the shore

...

We shared history both young and old
He knew more about me with more truth to unfold
He said don't you worry - Help is on the way
I know who you are - They led you astray

...

Thousands of miles from where I was born
This old gentleman knew we were torn
Torn from the truth
Our identity washed away
There are those who remember and tell stories of our betray

...

I had to travel to this country
Close to my ancestor's home
Just to learn that we are not all alone
That help is on the way
What kind of help - I did reply
He told me to think Biblical and trust in the Most High

I remember the story my mother told me about my great, great grandmother. She was more, more than just a slave. She came from Kings and Queens.

GREAT-GREAT GRANDMOTHER "MARY JANE OF JUDEA"

Judea –Yehuda - Yehuday (Dah)
Praised – Celebrated - Your meaning
So sweet - Her birth - Her beauty
Great -Great Grandmother so unique
Born in this historic land of Israel
Judah - Originally I speak
Knowing the territory of the Israelite
My great-great grandmother loved you
And for her heritage I will fight
I always wondered-why I sparked at the mountains so high
The quiet still - The peaceful will of untouched territories
With silent whispers
Stories fill my soul
As I watch Our Heavenly Father's beauty unfold
Yehuday (Yehudah) - Oh how so near Jerusalem - Bethlehem
Where our savior was born and shed his first tear
My life - My heritage from millions of miles torn
Defeat after defeat - Trying to wipe out our identity
Israel – Judah - Judea from the seas my dynasty remains
Migrating to Sudan survival at best - Life is contained
A country Northeastern Africa - In the Arab world Sudan rest
Nubia lost - Name change - After name change
Once Independent - A Kingdom of your own
Now I must leave you for Ethiopia is my home
As I join my Ethiopian Dynasty - My new family - My new home

The second oldest country to become officially - What we know
as Christian
In Christ - I must mention
From a Dynasty she came
Captured and taken to the West Indies - They changed her true name
Mary Jane they called her
Sold and controlled in Savannah, Georgia
America - America Yehuda now I belong
My life in India
My seed goes on
My Royal Great-Great Grandmother your capture brought you me
From Judea, Sudan, Ethiopia and The West Indies
Thank you Heavenly Father for Great-Great Grandmother
My History
My Legacy

WE ARE MORE

Sitting alone wondering - Trying to enlighten my spirits
For I know that this person whom I see in the mirror is
More than they say

...

This shell in which our soul rest is just our protection
Voice threw which we speak
Years living
Studying
Seeking but finding only the knowledge of others

...

Something inside tells me there's more
How do we find this more
Our identity not theirs
Our Creator creates beauty
But this world has led us to believe that it's not ours

...

Peace my spirit seeks
Love for all that's righteous
The Commandments we follow – Exodus 20
This is our beauty that lets us know that we are more

...

More than always being last
More than just their picture of slavery
More than just words that our own people have adopted
More than that which tries to destroy our soul
We are from the Tribe of Judah

The Holy Bible in all of its Transliterations; we are seen throughout. We must read for ourselves to see our true nature come out. We were lost but not forgotten for we are in the beginning and the end. We are the chosen, the sacred, for in the end we will win. Suffer we must for we chose our fate. We served their idols, worshiped their earthly kings, from their table we ate. We must search deep; for our soul know that we are great. Great is our Heavenly Father! We could never be last for our "King (I AM THAT I AM) is the Greatest!"

__John 8: 58__ **Jesus said unto them, Verily, verily, I say unto you, Before Abraham was, I Am.**

MESSIAH

How wonderful and blessed to have such an anointed one
Our Creator loved us so much
Although we sinned he still sent us his son
Messiah please teach us - Love us and carry us to the light
Help us understand that we must do right

...

We must follow the Saviors teachings so we can see
Everlasting joy and eternity

...

They changed his name and his physical appearance
They can't take the truth because it is within us

...

Turn down your music.
Don't go dancing tonight
No arguing or fighting
No cards or Bud-light

...

Open your bible in quiet delight
Read for yourself for your spirit shall light
The Messiah is about peace and healing the soul
Blessing the meek while we gracefully grow old

...

There is no one to blame if you turn away from him with might
He wants you even in your darkest night
Your soul shall be saved - True peace at last
Our Messiah loves us in-spite of our past

...

We are blessed with the greatest gift of all
Our heritage
Our birthright
We are Israel

...

We must read throughout our Bible for we shall see
That Israel is you and me
Blood of his Blood we are the chosen one
Read with understanding
Our life in the Messiah has just begun

They take our people into captivity while erasing all traces of our royal birth—making us forget our royal worth. We are subliminal prisoners of war on every side. They are stealing and enslaving the soul—thinking and planning trying to master our minds. Making us think that we are guilty when they committed the crime. Their mass deception is of every kind. You are innocent. Don't let them keep you blind. This is where they want you—that slave plantation mind...

MISLEAD

You're walking and talking and shaking your rump
Fooling young girls - That makes you a chump
Barely wearing clothes so you can be seen
Putting up signs like a devil worshiping queen
Flaunting gold chains thinking that makes you reign
Dealing with men that's acting like Cain
Following those you barely know name
Big sin, little sin - The results the same

...

You once knew the truth but your ego took control
You're disrespecting the Creator and acting so bold
Mislead by the power that you think you have
Misleading the young and old
You gave your soul to the devil
Because he gave you fool's gold

...

Taking the forbidden
Thinking your sins will be hidden
Receiving gifts that you think your soul has bought
Pretty soon you too will be caught
Your torment is only moments away
Because it is the Creator that you hurt and betrayed

...

Easily mislead
Eyes wide open
All for fame and fortune
You know the story of Adam and Eve
You know it's the same way they were deceived
But you took the offer anyway
You gladly smiled and cheerfully obeyed

...

Mislead - Now the price is on your head
Flee from the traps and stop your sinning
Read Genesis and remember what happened in the beginning
Do not continue to disrespect our Heavenly Father's grace
Do not use your free will to destroy what's left of your race

Genesis 6:5 "And God saw that the wickedness of man was great in the earth, and that every imagination of the thoughts of his heart was only evil continually. 6 And it repented the LORD that he had made man on the earth, and it grieved him at his heart. 7 And the LORD said, I will destroy man whom I have created from the face of the earth; both man, and beast, and the creeping thing, and the fowls of the air; for it repenteth me that I have made them. 8 But Noah found grace in the eyes of the LORD."

ARROGANCE

So you're still riding on your invisible magic carpet
Your pride taking you to invisible heights
Walking over the less fortunate
Selling all of your virtuous rights
Demanding much but giving little
Putting yourself on the Creator's throne
Mentally thinking you are at the top of it all
Your arrogance will make you fall

...

If you read the Bible like you say
Then you should have learned
So you say no man should have all that power
Referring to our Creator
For that saying - You have destined your final hour
Self-centered - Someone told you wrong
Deceiving the weak will never make you strong

...

You disrespected our Heavenly Father and acted like a scoffer
Just see what happens when they've taken all you have to offer
Here trying to protect you from yourself
For when the real souls see you all they see is an elf
Trickery - Destroying your soul and yours alone
Trying to change the Creators course
Pushing evil and the devils deeds
You fill your emptiness with arrogance
To think you know it all
You deceive - You transgress
You have created a deadly sinful mess
Flee from sin
Save your soul and repent

LINGUISTIC ME

Correcting and integrating our previous knowledge
We were never a slave - Nor our ancestors who wore collars
Pulled with chains and imprisoned with scholars
Integrated into a land whose vocabulary was unknown
Mastered by a man who kidnaped us from our throne

...

Premeditated - Was our phenomena
People were never meant to be the property of others
We were all created equal and are the same as our brothers

...

Our Heavenly Father created us in his own image
We belong to him - He created and started our lineage

...

Held against our will- From the time of our capture
They planned it to last until the foretold rapture
A true **Holocaust** was our experience with massive destruction
Humans destroying other Humans
Massive slaughters on ships
Hangings, burnings
While dead and buried under construction
When our story is told - They call it slavery so we won't prosper
When others are told it's a holocaust or war
So in our story - They think they will never settle the score

...

Now we must seek to understand this world's language
Young and old
Our words unfold
When not remarkable to their understanding
They call us ignorant and leave us hanging

...

We use slang because the English language was never our known
We create words for something to own
Our thirst for our own language our heart is missing
Linguistic Me - For I'm tracing our identity
Correcting our history and the story of our worth
With your help - We can discover our birth

CHAPTER 7
FREE WILL

FREE WILL - DON'T GO OVERBOARD
IT'S DANGEROUS WITHOUT YOUR LIFE PRESERVE
THERE IS ALWAYS A CONSEQUENCE FOR EVERY CHOICE
FOR EVERY VOICE
FOR EVERY DECISION WE MAKE
WHEN YOU ACTIVATE YOU FREE WILL
THINK - DWELL AND CONTEMPLATE

FREE WILL

Free will is a gift
Not to be misused and abused
Free will is a choice
Knowing what is right
Not going off course
Free will awakens the soul
So your spirit can decide
Free will was never meant to be overthrown with pride

...

Free will is never taking for granted the choice that's yours
Free will was never to be taken out of control

...

Free will, given at no cost
Free will, never meant to be taken into slavery

...

No choice to be made
Free will imprisoned
No price to be paid

...

Free will, not knowing it's there
Taken from you with mind control
Your knowledge was stripped
You've lost your script
Not knowing that you have the power

...

Free will is your strength
Its power only works with righteousness
Reaching spiritual heights
Gaining holy consciousness

...

Free will, working with the positive force
When evil exist - It silence your voice
So your ego takes control
Making decisions
Ending up in collisions
Not knowing how to unfold

DON'T USE YOUR FREE WILL TO DISRESPECT THE CREATOR:

DON'T DISRESPECT THE CREATOR

Don't disrespect the Creator
Don't disrespect our King
Check out the way you dress
You are supposed to represent Him in all things
...

You got dresses so short - You can't sit down
Blouses so low - Babies crying for milk
Your dress is see through - You forgot the silk
Pants sagging - Easy access
Walking around with a butt pass
Putting it out like you want cash
Subliminal - Say what
Pull your pants up – Stop showing your butt
You can't walk - You can't run - Because your butts out
Even the toddlers are wondering - What is that all about
...

You know the Creator is looking down on you
You show your dishonor in what you do
You say why the war, earthquakes, sickness and death
...

But did you ever think to look
At the rules he left in his book
The bible teaches us about honor
You walk around disrespecting our King
...

Mad at the world
But check out your part

Our Heavenly Father created us
Now we are breaking his heart
Check out the way you dress
Don't disrespect the Creator
Don't disrespect our King

WE MUST REPRESENT OUR HEAVENLY FATHER IN ALL THINGS!

MEDIA TAKE OUT

Media Take Out
At a restaurant near you
Short mini dresses and sagging pants
Dresses cut so low
Putting men and women in a trance
Trying to be a part of the in crowd
Not knowing that it doesn't make your parents proud
You say that your parents don't care
You're all alone
No one's home
You can do as you please

...

Our Heavenly Father created us in his own image
You say you have no respect for your earthly parents
You say it's your free will
You can do what you want to do
You clearly forgot about the one that created every inch of you
You need to check your level of respect
Even Satan himself bows down and our Heavenly Father keeps
him in check!
Don't sell your soul and disrespect his temple
For he has the greatest wrath
Don't continue to tread on his path

...

If you do his will
You will see his compassion
He will return you unto your inheritance in Hebrew fashion
Take out all the media influenced control devises
Anoint your soul with heavenly spices

The true Hebrew Israelite agenda
Electrifying so remember
Love and obey our Heavenly Father

Remember: Your free will does not mean that you can do what you want, when you want and how you want! **SO DON'T BE:**

NO NIGGER - NO MORE

No nigger no more and that's for sure
There is no pride in the word nigger
It's not endearing my brother and sister with color
Your race is dying with your endearing galore
What's up my nigga is what they said when they shot him
Don't you remember your ancestors who picked cotton
They would be ashamed knowing that you use the same words
Nigger is almost all they heard
They burned and hanged them when they spoke that word
Don't rap to me with nigga this - Nigga that
Don't sell me what's up nigga - Straighten your naps
How does that sound to the ears of your child
I guess you don't know - He is out running wild
Nigga – Negro – Nigger - What is on your mind
Don't be lost in the mud with swine
I heard a rap song just the other day
Don't you brothers have more positive words to say
Don't come at me with I am flipping the word over
Saying that it was once sacred – They used it to abuse
Not the same word
When you use words they stay in your mind
You may think you are twisting it but it keeps you lost in time
A time that we must let go
Believe it or not words make us grow
Grow into something good or evil
It's something you must break free from
Don't be medieval
Nigga keeps us on that plantation forever
For our minds it weakens and our soul loose its flavor
Wake up for you must let it go

It's their word - Definitely not ours for sure
We are the chosen - The true Israelites
We are much more - We must reach our true heights
No Nigger - No more
It's nothing galore
Don't tell me its slang
Meaning friend - Or homey
That's fake - That's false - The word Nigga -
Nigger is the true phony
Yes - I can go on and on but then I will be tooting their horn
Our Creator designed us to be much greater than that
We are his chosen - Don't ever forget

"NO NIGGER NO MORE AND THAT'S FOR SURE!"

MY BEAUTIFUL CHILD

My beautiful child they took you from your home
Starved you
Removed your clothing
Mistreated you
Sexually and mentally abused you
Sold you into a state of mind no man was ever meant to endure
Covering it up with deception
Not pure

...

My beautiful child all is not lost
For the bible states - They will pay the cost
Cost of your deception
Cost of your lives
Cost of your bodies they slashed with knives

...

My beautiful babies
We heard your cries
For your tears fill the rain and thundering skies

...

As the tornadoes raft swirl
And destroys their world
Where you have suffered for so many years
My beautiful babies dry your eyes for your roaring sounds we hear

WEEP LIKE A CHILD

For your sins are great
You ate from the evil one's plate
You committed fornication with the wicked ones
You party like your life has just begun
You perpetrated the biggest sins

...

Weep like a child
For it's coming to an end
From bitter to sweet
Sweet to bitter
Turn back now
Before your soul is too weak
The truth I speak

...

Their deceiving the meek
And taking the week
Not keeping any real promise
Temporary is your fortune
For a short period is your fame
For all that you have given
There will be nothing you will gain

...

Weep like a child
Humble and dear
Pray to our Heavenly Father
Forgiveness is here
Not on your terms
When deaths at your door
Weep like a child as never before

A great and trying journey has brought me to this point. Trials and tribulations, misunderstandings and miscalculations has opened my eyes and has freed my soul.

Since Marcus, I have learned how to let my spiritual wisdom guide me. I now use wisdom, knowledge and understanding when choosing my paths and making decisions. I now have a greater understanding of my free will. "Now I am living."
I have been given:

ANOTHER CHANCE

Once not knowing
Hoping all is well
Once living under other's spell

...

Once sick and in pain
Nothing the Doctors could cure
Prayer and faith worked
That's for sure

...

Time alone without obligation
Also helped me out of my negative situation
Tear after fear
Love brought me back
Now I am clear

...

Clear with understanding of knowing my birth
Was not a mere chance but a gift from heaven to earth
What do I say
What do I do

...

I present my life as a present to you
For you to understand that all is not lost
For you to believe in our Heavenly Host

...

For he carried me through the storms and kept me warm
For he watched over my young and kept them safe from harm
I hope you understand and see what I see
How through all of this our Heavenly Father has set me free

...

Free to be loved
Choose and give
Another chance to life
Another chance to live

CHAPTER 8
MY GIFT

MY GIFT

Thank you for your love
That has kept me never alone
For I feel your touch in my every bone

Thank you for your tender mercy
For my sins were many
You forgave me and still blessed me with plenty

Thank you for never leaving me
For your mercy and never giving up
For my sins were many and my thank you were few
My giving you Praise is long over due

INDIA

From the Indus River is your name
You merge into the Arabian Sea

...

Living Within is your meaning
As my soul is within me

...

Soul within Flesh
Still lessons to learn

...

For knowledge and wisdom
Your truth - You must earn

...

Providing key water sources
You think of others - I can see
You have researched your truth so splendidly

...

Living within - Traveling throughout the seas
My name has more meaning - Whether Greek or Persian
interchangeably
With or without a name - My soul still resides in me

...

Israel/Judah is my bloodline
Regardless of my name in time
As I continue to serve my Creator - The truly Divine

...

Understanding - The need to know more
India - My beauty has opened the door

Psalm 27:1-3 King James Version (KJV) The Lᴏʀᴅ is my light and my salvation; whom shall I fear? the Lᴏʀᴅ is the strength of my life; of whom shall I be afraid? ² When the wicked, even mine enemies and my foes, came upon me to eat up my flesh, they stumbled and fell.³ Though an host should encamp against me, my heart shall not fear: though war should rise against me, in this will I be confident.

WE ARE TAUGHT TO THINK THE WORST OF OURSELVES AND OUR RACE. WE ARE LOOKED DOWN ON BY THE MAJORITY OF FACES. WHEN ONE PERSON FROM OUR RACE DOES SOMETHING WRONG- OUR RACE AS A WHOLE IS JUDGED.

WE ARE PROFILED. WE ARE CALLED MANY NAMES REFERRING TO ANIMALS. **TO HAVE THAT MUCH HATE IS BARBAROUS.**

THEY TRY TO BELITTLE US BY TALKING ABOUT OUR SKIN COLOR/HAIR. THEY WANT THE MASSES TO THINK THAT THEY ARE PERFECT—THAT THEIR LIFE IS PERFECT. THEY MASK HATE ON EVERY SIDE.

THEY TAKE THEIR ENERGY/TIME AND FOCUS IT ON OUR RACE
TO JUDGE - TREAT CRUEL AND IN HUMAN
KARMA – FATE – WHAT GOES AROUND COMES AROUND
DO UNTO OTHERS AS YOU HAVE THEM DO UNTO YOU
THEY THINK NONE OF THIS APPLIES TO THEM AND WONDER
WHY WARS – EARTHQUAKES - TORNADOES ETC.
THE WRATH OF OUR HEAVENLY FATHER IS WORST THAN
THAT OF MAN
WHEN HIS ELECT AND CHOSEN ARE HURT AND DESTROYED
THE GREAT "I AM THAT I AM" FEELS OUR PAIN
THE PAIN OF OUR ANCESTORS - HIS WRATH CAN NOT BE
ESCAPED

Galatians 6:7 Be not deceived; God is not mocked: for whatsoever a man soweth, that shall he also reap.

YOU MURDERED - YOUNG AND OLD - MOLESTED AND RAPED
THEY SAY GO BACK TO AFRICA
I SAY YOU BROUGHT US HERE
YOU TAKE US BACK - ALIVE - THE WAY YOU CAPTURED US
NOPE – TO LATE – OUR HEAVENLY FATHER WILL INITIATE
PEOPLE OF COLOR WAS IN THIS COUNTRY BEFORE THE EUROPEANS
IT'S A FACT - DO YOUR RESEARCH
AND IT WASN'T JUST THE INDIANS
HEBREW ISRAELITES WERE HERE AS WELL
THE TRUE ELITE KNOW THIS
THAT IS HOW YOU CAN TELL AN INTELLIGENT PERSON
FROM AN IGNORANT ONE
**THE ONES THAT KNOW OF OUR ROYAL STATUS ARE ON THE
SIDELINES MAKING MILLIONS – BILLIONS - TRILLIONS**

THE ONES THAT DO THE DIRTY DEEDS LACK THE KNOWLEDGE AND ARE BARBAROUS BECAUSE IF THEY KNEW THAT THEY WERE TAMPERING WITH A SACRED PEOPLE--THEY WOULD NOT CONTINUE THEIR BARBAROUS WAYS IN THE NAME OF THEIR JUSTICE. THE SELLING OF THE SOUL CAN PUT ONE REGARDLESS OF RACE IN A BARBAROUS STATE.

MANY OF OUR PEOPLE HAVE TURNED AGAINST THEIR OWN TO BE ON THE POPULAR/MAJORITY AGENDA. THERE IS ONLY ONE SIDE FOR ME AND THAT IS THAT OF THE HEAVENLY FATHER! DIFFERENT TRIBES SAME SOURCE - WAKE UP PEOPLE! IT'S A JUNGLE OUT HERE–LET THE BUYER BEWARE!

MATTHEW 7:15 BEWARE OF FALSE PROPHETS, WHICH COME TO YOU IN SHEEP'S CLOTHING, BUT INWARDLY THEY ARE RAVENING WOLVES. KJV

RHYTHM AND RHYME

Presenting the facts of the United Nations
With various topics from Hip Hop Relations
Relevant to all - Not joint in task
Indications of war - Beyond our control
That's why your lyrics
You must unfold

...

Enforcing Resolutions of Rhythm and Rhyme
Rapping to each beat - One at a time

...

No legal Requirements for your words to flow
Peace - Not war - Only your words can show

...

Seeing is believing
Your hearing not alone
Put it on paper and give a home

...

We talk about the crisis all over the world
Pollution - No solution in your mind you must see
The lyrical genius in you and me
So give it some thought and your words will soon flow
Seeking Peace - Not War - For all to know

THANK YOU

Praises to you my great and mighty King
From your throne you created every thing
My praises to you comes with soul felt meaning
Spirit and praise all through my days

Thank you for your creation
Your beauty I see
When I look at the sky and stare at the tree

Thank you for your love
That has kept me never alone
For I feel your touch in my every bone

Thank you for your tender mercy
For my sins were many
You forgave me and still blessed be with plenty

Thank you for never leaving me
For your mercy and never giving up
For my sins were many and my thank you were few
My giving you Praise is long over due

Thank you for your greatness
For it shines in the night
Through my every trial and weakest flight
Your love has kept me safe
Thank you for never leaving me alone is this place
Thank you for your sincere and everlasting grace

DEFINITIONS FROM NOAH WEBSTER'S 1828 DICTIONARY

(Noah Webster's 1828 Dictionary is said to contains the greatest number of Biblical definitions given in any reference volume)

1. American: a. Pertaining to America
American, n. A native of America; originally applied to the aboriginals, or copper-colored races, found here by the Europeans; but now applied to the descendants of Europeans born in America.

2. Barbarous: a. Uncivilized; savage; unlettered; untutored; ignorant; unacquainted with arts; stranger to civility of manners, Thou are a roman; be not barbarous.
2. Cruel; ferocious; inhuman; as barbarous.

3. Hebrew: n. [Heb. Eber, either a proper name, or a name denoting passage, pilgrimage, or coming from beyond the Euphrates.]
One of the descendants of Eber or Heber; but particularly, a descendant of Jacob, who was a descendant of Eber; an Israelite; a Jew.

4. Israelite: n. A descendant of Israel or Jacob; a Jew

5. Jew: n, [a contraction of Judas of Judah] A Hebrew or Israelite.

6. Niggard: n. [straight, narrow; to haggle, to be sordidly parsimonious: exhibiting analogies similar to those of wretch, wretch and haggle.] A miser; a person meanly close and covetous; a sordid wretch who saves every cent or spends grudgingly.

7. Shemitic: a. Pertaining to Shem, the son of Noah. The Shemetic language are Chaldee, Syriac, Arabic, Hebrew, Samaria, Ethiopic and Old Phoenician.

8. Slave: *n. 1. A person who is wholly subject to the will of* another; one who has no will of his own, but whose person and services are wholly under the control of another. In the early state of the world, and to this day among some **barbarous** nations, prisoners of war are considered and treated as slaves. The slaves of modern times are more generally purchased, like horses and oxen.

2. One who has lost the poser of resistance; or one who surrenders himself to any power whatever; as a slave to passion, to lust, to ambition.

3. A mean person; one in the lowest sate of life.

4. A drudge; one who labors like a slave.

9. Slave Trade: n. [slave and trade.] The **barbarous** and wicked business of purchasing men and women, transporting them to a distant country and selling them for slaves.

BIBLIOGRAPHY

1. Arab slave ship intercepted by the Royal Navy 1869. "This image (or other media file) is in the public domain because its copyright has expired." Wikimedia Commons.
2. Beard, Jos. A. Valuable Gang of Young Negroes 1840 Advertising Poster. "This image is in the public domain because its copyright has expired." Wikimedia Commons.
3. Houghton, Henry & Mifflin, George 1982/1985. Definition of Black/White as quoted by: Second College Edition of The American Heritage Dictionary. Houghton Mifflin Company – Boston.
4. King James Reference Bible (Authorized King James Version). [Bible Scriptures] Copyright 2000 by Zondervan.
5. Kordas. Twelve Tribes of Israel Map. GNU Free Documentation License. 12_tribus_de_Israel.svg. Creative Commons – Wikimedia Commons.
6. Luca. Phoenician Alphabet. "I Luca grants anyone the right to use this work for any purpose, without any conditions, unless such conditions are required by law." Wikimedia Commons.
7. Mathers, S. L. MacGregor (published prior to 1922). The media file is in the public domain in the United States. The copyright has expired. Wikimedia Commons.
8. Megistias. The World as Known to the Hebrews: A map from "Historical Textbook and Atlas of Biblical Geography (1854)" by Coleman. Wikimedia Commons.
9. Pyle, Justin D. (2003 TSGT, USAF). Goree Island, Senegal located off the Western African coast. "This image or file is a work of a U.S. Air Force Airman or employee, taken or made during the course of the person's official duties. As a work of the U.S. Federal Government, the image or file is in the public domain." Wikimedia Commons.

10. Pyle, Justin D. (2003 TSGT, USAF). Inside the Masion des Esclaves (Slave House) location: Goree Island, Senegal. "This image is a work of the U.S. Military or Department of Defense employee, taken or made during the course of an employee's official duties. As a work of the U.S. Federal Government, the image is in the public domain." Wikimedia Commons.

11. Quadell at en.wikipedia. Slave ship poster. "This image (or media file) is in the public domain because its copyright has expired." Wikimedia Commons.

12. Quasipalm. Early Historical Israel Map. "This work has been release into the Public domain by its author, Quasipalm. Quasipalm grants anyone the right to use this work for any purpose, without any conditions, unless such conditions are required by law." Wikimedia Commons.

13. Richardprins (2010 UTC). Kingdoms of Israel and Judah Map. GNU Free Documentation License. Creative Commons – Wikimedia Commons.

14. Richards, Wm. T.J. $100 Bounty for runaway slave image. "This media file is in the public domain in the United States. This applies to US. works where the copyright has expired, often because its first publication occurred prior to January 1, 1923." Wikimedia Commons.

15. Scholar, Neo. Hebrew Alphabet (Created using character map and the gimp). September 6, 2008. "I, the copyright holder of this work, release this work into the public domain. I grant anyone the right to use this work for any purpose, without any conditions, unless such conditions are required by law."

16. U.S. Federal Government. Slave Population 1860 Map. "This work is in the public domain in the United States because it is a work of the United States Federal Government under the terms of Title 17, Chapter 1, Section 105 of the U.S. Code." Wikimedia commons.

17. Webster, Noah. Definitions from Noah Webster's 1828 Dictionary. http://www.1828-dictionary.com/d/search/word,black.

18. Zbikowski, Conrad. Chart of the growth of the slave population and cotton production in the United States. "I, the copyright holder of this work, hereby release it into the public domain. I grant anyone the right to use this work for any purpose, without any conditions, unless such conditions are required by law." Wikimedia Commons.

TRUE IDENTITY

A Spiritual Poetry Inheritance

"True Identity" is not your average book of poetry because the poetry is connected to stories, biblical scriptures, art and images.

Since I was a little girl, I was into poetry. I wrote about everything that I saw going on. Why? I was trying to understand this world that we live in. I was trying to understand the who, what, why, when, where and how. I feel that we must seek truth. Our life, our true identity! Most races can trace their history but we (so-called Blacks) hold on to the voyage of slavery as if that's our only legacy. Well, I'm here to tell you it's not my friend.